THE JOY OF LIVING

The Secret of Finding and Keeping Happiness in Your Life

Dr. Orison Swett Marden

introduction

In the 1970s, a group of men some of the most influential motivational writers and speakers, including W. Clement Stone, Earl Nightingale, Norman Vincent Peale, and Og Mandino, were eating dinner in Chicago after one of the Positive Thinking Rallies sponsored by *Success* magazine. Someone raised the question, "Who have been the most influential nonfiction authors in your life?"

W. Clement Stone said "Orison Swett Mareden and Napoleon Hill."
Earl Nightingale said "Fyodor Dostoyevsky and Marden."
Norman Vincent Peale said, "The Scriptures and Marden."
Og Mandino said, "James Allen, Russel Conwell, and Marden."

Who is this man, Orison Swett Marden, who had such a profound influence on some of the greatest motivational speakers and writers of the twentieth Century? To further acquaint you with the man, here's a brief biography, written by the editors of *Success* magazine:

> Orison Swett Marden rose from wretched poverty to become the number one evangelist of entrepreneurship in his day. Marden was born in 1850, in rural, rugged New Hampshire. His mother died when Orison was three, his father when he was seven. His guardian wasted no time sending him off as a hired boy. Over the next decade, Marden worked for a series of rural New Hampshire families engaged in surveying, carpentry, mills, and farms—and most treated him terribly.
>
> He would spend his days hauling rocks until his hands bled, his night washing and scrubbing until his fingers screamed with pain. He

was regularly whipped, beaten, kicked, and nearly starved. He stayed for one year with a mean-spirited parson and his wife, where he ached with hunger and was forced to spend hours praying in a bleak, ramshackle church. Between the man and his wife, Orison was beaten almost every day. Marden recalled with a touch of humor that he was sometimes spared a whipping when the couple would argue over whose turn it was to beat him!

Through his teen years, Marden had lived entirely in the back woods. He had never read a newspaper or magazine, seen a crowd of more than 50 people, never seen a library, and had no concept of a city. He did love to read, however. He found a book, in the attic of one of the farms, that would change his life. It was *Self Help* by Samuel Smiles, a Scottish doctor, newspaper editor, and secretary for a railroad. Published in 1859 in England, *Self Help* told stories of boys who had pulled themselves up by their bootstraps from dire circumstances. Smiles declared that people could rise above their circumstances and achieve whatever they set their minds to do, if they would only exercise unshakable persistence and a positive mental attitude. It had sold over 250,000 copies by the turn of the century.

From the inspiration of *Self Help*, Marden left his legal guardian at age 17 and went on to get an education. He spent hours each day working, as a waiter and later a manager of several hotels, to feed himself, while he studied late at night to improve his learning and reading abilities. He worked his way through New London Academy, Boston University, Harvard University Medical School, and Boston University Law School (earning his last two degrees simultaneously in 1882). He embarked on an entrepreneurial career founding restaurants and eating clubs, buying hotels and real estate, and founded Success magazine.

Along the way, Marden decided to become the Samuel Smiles of America and write dozens of self-help books to inspire people to greatness. Financially secure by age 32, he spent his spare time collecting notes of "inspiration and help to strugglers trying to be somebody and do something in the world." According to scholar Tom Lutz, Marden combined the values outlined by Ben Franklin—

economy, self-control, work, and honesty—with those later set down by Ralph Waldo Emerson—self-reliance, sagacity, and truth—to define a potent and uniquely American philosophy.

Beginning in 1890, Marden was hit with a series of disasters. A smallpox outbreak ruined his business at one of his hotels. A drought dried up all his business in the West. All of his writings (some 5,000 pages) were destroyed in a fire in another of his hotels. Undaunted and armed with his forward-looking attitude, Marden bought himself a 25-cent notebook the next morning and started to write all over again.

He began to reconstruct his favorite manuscript, *Pushing to the Front*, which told the stories of great men who began, often in abject poverty, struggled in the face of repeated discouragement, and triumphed in the end. Published in 1891 by Houghton-Mifflin, the book was a widely translated and influential best-seller, and it helped to turn his life around both financially and emotionally. He received such enthusiastic letters in response that he decided to form *Success* magazine. In *Success*, Marden sought to inspire and uplift, to teach and to hold up models of success as a beacon for others who aspired to be the same. He interviewed the most successful and powerful people of his day, and the magazine carved a unique niche for itself in American society. Marden edited the magazine until his death in 1924.*

Happiness was compiled from many of the writings of Marden's. In his writings, Marden often referred to the works of others—many are well-known to this day; others have faded from popular familiarity. Some references to the latter have been left in this book. This was based on the decision that their words illumined the text in a way that added to the meaning, imagery, and elegance of the text. Though their names are no longer familiar and their identities obscure, you will nonetheless acquire an acquaintance of them by their words. And in the final analysis, it's by their words that ultimately they wanted to be known.

Sometimes Marden simply inserted quoted passages into his writings without any reference to the source. Again, where these added contextual richness to the material, they have been left in.

In both instances, the decision was made that you would profit more and your reading experience be made greater by knowing these writers' words —even if you didn't know or weren't familiar with their names—than you would if their words were not included.

At the end of each chapter, there is a section entitled "Today I Will ..." This is followed by several suggested activities that you can begin doing in order to bring a greater degree and quality of happiness into your life. These suggested activities were not part of Marden's original writings. They have been added with the hope that they will enrich your ability to acquire benefit in your life from this book. In some instances, the suggestions are short sentences. Others are followed by explanations regarding the meaning and purpose of the suggestion. The first sentence of every suggested activity is written in the first person, as it is to complete the heading "Today I will ..." If there is an explanation afterwards, it is in the third-person, addressing you.

Following these suggestions, there are several blank lines. These are places where you can write your own ideas for activities you would like to begin. These spaces were included in this book because the suggested activities are just that: suggestions. Their intention as suggestions is two-fold: as activities suggested as possible practices you will want to incorporate into your life, and as creative ideas that may suggest to you further activities of your own choosing. Put into practice the suggested activities if you wish and add your own, or use the suggested activities as creative resources for designing your own activities. This is your book, about your life, and only you know the types of activities that will open your life to greater happiness.

Enjoy ... and be happy.

---

* Short biography by Scott DeGarmo, with contributions from Don Wallace and historical research by Enid Klass. Much of this material appeared in a special 23-page insert in *Success* (November 1991), commemorating the 100th anniversary of the magazine.

chapter 1

THE HUNT FOR HAPPINESS

"Oh, thou that pinest in the imprisonment of the actual and criest bitterly to the gods for a kingdom wherein to rule, know this truth: the thing thou seekest is already with thee, here or nowhere, couldst thou only see."

We were made to be happy. It is a mighty motive in every human being. From infancy on, the desire for fun, for amusement, for play, for joys that endure, is very strong in each of us. If the majority of the people in the world were asked to express their three greatest wishes, they would ask for health, wealth, and happiness. And if they were then told to state their *supreme* wish in life, the majority would ask for happiness.

But how few of us have ever find true happiness, and we have not because of how we have sought it: Like looking for a needle in a haystack, most of us not only do not know *where* to look for happiness, but *how* to even begin looking. And so we have made a specialty of *hunting* for happiness. But happiness is not gained that way. It is not to be found by hunting, as hunters hunt for wild animals. No one has ever found happiness by chasing after it over the earth. It is not in our food, it is not in our drink, it is not in our clothes or material possessions; it is not in excitement or a constant round of amusements and "having a good time." It is not in the titillation of the nervous system. It does not come from the gratification of desires or of possessions.

Nonetheless, somehow most people seem to think that happiness can be found just as people find gold—and that likewise, that there is a great deal of luck about it.

Everywhere we see people trying to get something that somebody else has which they think would add to their happiness if they could only get hold of it. But piling things around you, no matter how high, can never make you happy.

Those who are always hunting for something which will make them happy, some indulgence which will gratify their cravings are always disappointed seekers. Often too late, they realize that the pursuit of our cravings only increase our real soul-hunger, that "desire is as insatiable as the ocean, and clamors louder and louder as its demands are attended to."

Happiness is the product of a mental attitude. It will do you no good to chase all over the world trying to find happiness. If you not carry it with you, you will never find it. History is strewn with wrecks of those who pursued happiness desperately all their lives and never once caught up with it.

If we chase after happiness, then we must remember that wherever we search for it, we will only find what we take with us of ourselves.

This means that happiness can never be found outside ourselves. The whole philosophy of the Bible emphasizes this fact: the kingdom of heaven —by which is meant the kingdom of happiness—is *within* us. Yet, in all times, the great majority of people have been hunting for a kingdom of happiness that is *without*, not within themselves at all.

Real happiness is attained by worthy service to others—by trying to do our part in the world, by the desire to be helpful, and by making the world a better place to live in because of our efforts.

Real happiness comes not from searching outside, but from listening within. It comes from keeping foremost in our attention that in fact, in the final analysis, our innermost longings are for the simplest, the quietest, the most unpretentious things in the world: sunsets, friendships, quiet walks, flowers, moonlight, little kindnesses, pleasant words, little helps by the way, little encouragements, love, and affection.

Our real happiness cannot be found anywhere else.

Today I will...

→ *Stop looking for happiness and instead find it where I am.*

→ *Remind myself that if I am going to search for happiness, the place to search for it is within myself. If your life is not as happy as you'd like it to be, if you are not as happy as you'd like to be, the happiness you're longing for is not hidden someplace outside of you, it's gotten lost someplace inside of you. Look within to find out what it is that is locking up your happiness.*

→ *Remind myself that real happiness is not found by frantically searching for the perfect outfit to wear on a date (to an outing, for a meeting, etc.). Too often, we get caught up in thinking that happiness is in finding, obtaining, or grasping onto something that we don't have (e.g., a nicer home to invite a new friend or a new person we like over to for dinner). "If only I had _____" (whatever), we say, then we'd be happy. How much happiness do you take away from yourself by thinking it is already something you lack?*

→ _____

→ _____

→ _____

→ _____

chapter 2

HAPPINESS CAN BE CULTIVATED

There is no duty we under-rate as the duty of being happy.
—Robert Louis Stevenson

Few people realize that happiness may be cultivated. They seem to think that the power to enjoy life is largely hereditary, that they cannot do very much to change their dispositions. Indeed, when referring to their own or another's character, they often speak of their or the other's "nature"—as if their character were something intrinsic, invariable.

But we *can* learn, we *can* change, we *can* grow.

When the world was young, the human brain was very primitive, because the demand upon it was largely for self-protection and the acquisition of food; but gradually a higher call was made upon it, a more varied development demanded, and now it has became exceedingly complex. Every new demand of civilization has made a new call upon the brain, and it has responded to the call and has adapted itself to modern needs.

Our brain is very adaptable, as shown by the effects upon it by the different vocations we engage in. Each interest that we have makes a different call upon the brain, and the brain, accordingly, develops faculties and characteristics peculiar to that interest. In other words, the brain changes to meet the demand made upon it. It is modified by the various activities and motives which we call upon it for in order to handle the conditions which we have to meet in life.

For example, take courage. Many successful people were, as children, so completely devoid of this quality that it threatened to wreck their careers.

Their courage was strengthened through the help of intelligent training—the cultivation of self-confidence, the constant holding in the mind the suggestion of courage, the contemplation of brave deeds.

Nonetheless, while most people acknowledge that it's true that developing a specialty in a career requires years in preparing for it, while they allow that certain character traits like courage can be learned, they persist in the conviction that one must relegate the attainment of happiness, which means more to them than almost anything else, to the status of haphazard development—believed to come, if it comes at all, without any required no training or no special study, while everything else in life that is worth while requires such infinite pains. They forget that most unhappy people have gradually become so by forming the habit of unhappiness. The habit of complaining, of criticizing, of faultfinding or grumbling over trifles, the habit of looking for shadows, is one most unfortunate to contract, especially in early life, for after a while one becomes a slave to it.

I know a lady who once underwent an operation for the removal of a tumor. Everything in her life dates from that time. She cannot converse on any subject but she drags in her "operation." It is her excuse for her explanation of all her shortcomings in domestic affairs.

How many people are loath to let their troubles go! They have lived with them so long that they have become sort of companions, and they seem to take a morbid pleasure in entertaining them, in displaying them and going over them every opportunity they have.

One of the most difficult lessons of life is to learn that we are largely the product of our thought; that our environment, our education, our habitual thought have very much more to do with the output of our lives than heredity. St. Paul was really scientific when he said to his disciples: "Be ye transformed by the renewing of your mind."

We can so educate the willpower that it will focus the thoughts upon the bright side of things—upon objects which elevate the soul, thus forming a habit of happiness and goodness which will enrich the whole life.

"Happiness," says an able writer, "is the greatest paradox in nature. It can grow in any soil, live under any conditions. It defies environment because it comes from within. Happiness consists not of having, but of being; not of possessing, but of enjoying. While what a person *has*, he or she may be dependent on others; what a person *is*, rests with himself or herself alone. What one *ob*tains in life is but acquisition; what one *at*tains, is growth.

"Happiness is the warm glow of a heart at peace with itself. A martyr at the stake may have happiness that a king on his throne might envy. Man is the creator of his own happiness; it is the aroma of a life lived in harmony with high ideals. Happiness is the soul's joy in the possession of the intangible."

It is the duty of everybody to cultivate a happy, joyful nature, a kindly eye, the power of radiating good will toward every one. It will not only brighten the lives of others, but the reflex action of such kindly effort will also help to develop that exquisite personality, that beauty of character and balance of soul, that serenity, which is the greatest wealth we know.

"Be glad!" exclaims a helpful writer. "When you have said all there is to say about life's sorrow, disappointment, and pain, about the selfishness and wrong that sweep over the earth like dark shadows, about the shortness of its days and the certainty of its nights, it still remains blessedly true that the universe is thrilling with the song of gladness."

One of the best of success helps is to acquire—and the earlier in youth possible, the better—a habit of thinking that the best, not the worst, will happen; that we are not poor, miserable creatures, hounded on every hand by the enemies of our life and happiness, but that we were made to be free from harassing cares, anxieties, forebodings—not made to worry.

"Cultivate a philosophical vein of thought," recommends Ella Wheeler Wilcox. "If you have not what you like, like what you have until you can change your environment."

"Do not waste your vitality in hating your life; find something in it which is worth liking and enjoying, while you keep steadily at work to make it what you desire. Be happy over something, every day, for the brain is a thing of habit, and you cannot teach it to be happy in a moment, if you allow it to be miserable for years."

We should no more allow a discordant or a dark picture in the mind—whether of fear, worry, selfishness, hatred, or jealousy—than we would allow a thief in our home. We should remember that such thoughts are worse than thieves, because they steal away our comfort, our happiness, our contentment. We should learn that these enemies have no right to intrude themselves upon our consciousness. Treat them as trespassers, eject them instantly, and do not allow them to paint their despairing images upon the mind. For it is almost impossible to exclude them when they once enter, but it is comparatively easy to keep them out when we once learn the secret of excluding them.

And what is that secret? It is this: Those who are habitually sad or gloomy are so because the corresponding thoughts predominate their minds. By simply thinking the opposite thoughts, they could produce the opposite results. Our state of mind is largely a mental habit which is not very difficult to change.

The story is told of an elderly woman, the widow of a soldier who had been killed in the Civil War, who went to a photographer's to have her picture taken. She was seated before the camera wearing the same stern, hard, forbidding look that had made her an object of fear to the children living in the neighborhood, when the photographer, thrusting his head out from the black cloth, said suddenly, "Brighten the eyes a little."

She tried, but the dull and heavy look still lingered.

"Look a little pleasanter," said the photographer, in an unimpassioned but confident and commanding voice.

"See here," the woman retorted sharply, "if you think that an old woman who is dull can look bright, that one who feels cross can become pleasant every time she is told to, you don't know anything about human nature. It takes something from the outside to brighten one up."

"Oh, no, it doesn't! *It's something you can work from the inside.* Try it again," said the photographer, good-naturedly.

His tone and manner inspired faith, and she tried again, this time with better success.

"That's good! That's fine! You look twenty years younger," exclaimed the artist, as he caught the transient glow that illuminated the faded face.

She went home with a queer feeling in her heart. It was the first compliment she had received since her husband had passed away, and it left a pleasant memory. When she reached her little cottage, she looked long in the glass. "There may be something in it," she said, "but I'll wait and see the picture."

When the photograph came, it was like a resurrection. The face seemed alive with the lost fires of youth. She gazed long and earnestly, then said in a clear, firm voice, "If I could do it once, I can do it again."

Approaching the little mirror above her bureau, "Brighten up, Catherine," she said, and the old light flashed up once more.

"Look a little pleasanter!" she commanded; and a calm and radiant smile diffused itself over her face.

Her neighbors soon remarked the change that had come over her: "Why, Mrs. A, you are getting young! How do you manage it?"

"It is all done from the inside. You just brighten up inside and feel pleasant."

Every emotion tends to sculpture the body into beauty or into ugliness. Worrying, fretting, unbridled passions, petulance, discontent, every dishonest act, every falsehood, every feeling of envy, jealousy, fear—each has its effect on the system, and acts deleteriously like a poison or a deformer of the body. Professor Henry James of Harvard, an expert in the mental sciences, says, "Every small stroke of virtue or vice leaves its ever so little scar. Nothing we ever do is, in strict literalness, wiped out."

The way to be beautiful without is to be beautiful within.

No one can be really happy or successful unless he or she learns how to become the master of his or her moods. And the key is the knowledge that you yourself are a power back of the brain, that you are in charge of the human machine, is a wonderful aid to self-control and happiness.

Do you, who say you cannot control your temper, that the explosion comes before you have time to think? Ever consider that your brain is not *you*; that it is absolutely within your control; that this great human machinery is outside the mind; that you can control every thought and be master of every emotion, with proper training—so that your machine will never run wild, the brain never race away with you?

You are the person behind the brain.

Test this in your life. Notice that there are some people in whose presence you never would think of losing self-control, no matter what, the provocation? There is somebody whose very presence would keep you from losing your bearings under the most provoking circumstances. All of us know some man or woman, or have some friend, before whom nothing in the world could move us beyond our self-control. On the other hand, before an employee, upon whom we might look as simply a part of the machinery of our business, for whom we have no real regard or sympathy, or at home, where we may feel little restraint, we lose his temper at the slightest provocation. This proves that we can control ourselves to an infinitely greater extent than we seem to think. The most explosive-tempered person would not show anger at a reception or dinner to distinguished persons, no matter what the fancied insult might be. He or she would not think of such a thing. If we had the proper regard for every one, if we respected even the humblest human being, as we ought to, and respected ourselves sufficiently, we should have little trouble in controlling ourselves.

"If you think of it and reflect upon it often, happiness will become habitual and a power in your hands for so much good," says Margaret Stowe. "We can cultivate the habit of always looking on the bright side of things. We all possess the power of exercising the will so as to direct the thoughts upon objects calculated to yield to happiness and improvement rather than their opposites.

"If we try always to look happy and pleasant, whether we feel so or not, the effort will gradually become a habit with us."

We can form this habit of happiness by starting out making the most of little pleasures—not waiting for overwhelming joys. Many of us fail take time to enjoy the pleasant things in life. We trample down the violets and the beautiful small flowers trying to reach the larger life blossoms. We try too hard to attain the big things while it is the multitude of little things, the little enjoyments as we go along, that makes life happy.

It is our straining for big results that incapacitates us from enjoying the everyday little things—that keeps most of us from getting one-tenth of the blessings out of the present moment that are awaiting us.

"It is only now and then that a comet flashes into view, but the sunshine is a daily blessing," some one said, "and it would be a silly plant which waited for a comet to appear before putting forth blossoms. There is little likelihood that any extraordinary joy will come to you today, but there will be plenty of small pleasures. Make the most of each one. Enjoy the friendly letter which came in the morning's mail, the comfortable room in which you do your work, the pleasant acquaintance you made at dinner, the chance you had to say an encouraging word to the homesick co-worker in the next office. There is no mystery about happiness, neither is it a matter of chance, as some would have us think. Instead it is one of the most practical things in the world, and one who has learned to make the most of little everyday blessings has mastered its chief secret."

You may think that the routine of your life is extremely common, insipid, flavorless. But it does not necessarily mean that life is disappointing just because it has not measured up to the rosy pictures of your youthful dreams; it means that you have not formed the habit of happiness, and so have not learned to appreciate your life as it is passing. Right alongside of you there may be others who lead the same kind of a life you do but who are getting happiness out of it. Do you not hear others in your workplace or who are in your identical living conditions laughing boisterously? They find a way to make play of their circumstance, while you make sadness. They may find joy in it while you find nothing interesting in it.

How often, however, we hear people give expression to the thought that they don't get much out of life. Now this very spirit of trying to see how much they can get *out of* life is what causes them to get so little. It is the people who put the most *into* life that get the most out of it. A farmer might as well sit still and see how much he can get out of his farm without sowing and planting. It is the people who *give* the most to life who get the most out of it. With many people, life seem instead something to plunder rather than to cultivate to the utmost.

Just like the farmer who would till a particular piece of land from which he is trying to win a prize, you must put as much as you can into life, make it just as rich as possible. Put love and contentment into it, cheerfulness and unselfish service, then you will not go around complaining that you get so little out of life, that the world has no reward to offer you.

Real happiness comes from the cultivation, the development, of the highest that is in us. Selfishness can never bring happiness, because it is constantly developing, enlarging the greedy, grasping nature, is constantly encouraging the very thing which leads us away from happiness. You will not find happiness unless you see it with a pure heart, with a clean mind, a noble purpose, with unselfish aim and unselfish desire for the welfare of others.

The happiness habit is as necessary to our best welfare as the work habit or any other habit, and it is a great thing so to cultivate the art of happiness that we can get pleasure out of the common experiences of every day.

What a great thing it is indeed to be able to habitually turn one's back to every shadow that approaches, to face the light, whether much or little!

Nothing contributes more to the highest success than the formation of a habit of seeing the bright side of things. Whatever your calling in life may be, whatever misfortunes or hardships may come to you, make up your mind resolutely that, come what may, you will get the most possible real enjoyment out of every day; that you will increase your capacity for enjoying life, by trying to find the sunny side of every experience of the day. Resolutely determine that you will see the humorous side of things. No matter how hard or unyielding your environment may seem to be, there is a sunny side if you can only see it. The mirth-provoking faculty, even under trying circumstances, is worth more than the accumulation of a great fortune without it. Make up your mind that you will be an optimist, that there shall be nothing of the pessimist about you, that you will carry your own sunshine wherever you go.

Suppose the way *does* look dark to you; that you see no light, no opening. Do not take it for granted that there is no way out for you; that you will have no way to express what is locked up in you just because you happen to be temporarily tied to an iron environment and see now way of getting away from it in this moment. Wait, and work, and have faith. Don't waste your time on vain despair. Cultivate happiness. Remember, the closing of one door always means the opening of another.

Cultivate happiness as an art or science.

Be just as much ashamed of being unhappy as of being unwashed.

Today I will…

→ *Begin each morning by resolving to find something in the day to enjoy in happiness. Look within each experience which comes to you for some grain of happiness. You will be surprised to find how much that has seemed hopelessly disagreeable possesses either an instructive or an amusing side.*

- *Give attention to how much I have to be happy for. No matter what woes you have in your life, in this moment you also have the same stars, sun, and moon overhead as anyone whom you think is happier—you have the same opportunities to enjoy beauty; you have the same opportunities to meet someone anew and begin a friendship, a romantic relationship; you had the same opportunity to purchase this book; you have a roof over your head, a warm home, and running water just as they.*

- *Remind myself that if I am not as happy as I would wish to be, I am the one who is holding me back; today I will dwell on happiness instead of misfortune. "There is nothing either good or bad, but thinking makes it so" (Shakespeare). No matter how meager you think your surroundings are, there are many in the world who would envy what you have, the opportunities you have. Look around and you remind yourself of all that you have to be happy for that would make so many others in the world happy if they had it in their lives. Maybe it's nothing more than just having running water in your home, a warm shower always available to you, a radio where you can summon forth all the great singers and musicians of today, and yesterday, to provide your life with music to soothe your every mood.*

- *Remember that happiness is not obtained only from great events. One doesn't need a yacht, a summer home at the beach, or frequent excursions abroad in order to be a happy person. Many are happy who have not only never possessed any of these things, they've never seen them. Happiness can come from taking the time to play with your or your neighbor's pet; from taking the time to stop and talk with a child; from growing a garden and seeing the day come when the flowers on the table are those you watered and cared for—the vegetables are those you nurtured into their ripeness; from calling a friend and going for a bicycle ride together, or taking a walk, or going on a drive to some new place.*

- *Remember that happiness doesn't have to come from "doing" anything. Happiness can mean just giving yourself the afternoon to read that book you've been putting off reading; to going to a park and meditating; to staying home and finally cleaning out the garage, the attic, the basement, your home office—whatever—that you've been promising yourself you'd do.*
- *Make up my mind to be happy, to think of the best instead of the worst, remembering what Abraham Lincoln said: "Most folks are as happy as they make up their minds to be."*

- _____
- _____
- _____
- _____

chapter 3

AFFIRMATIONS AND HEART TALKS

*I am that which I think I am—
and I can be nothing else.*

A prominent music master in New York who trains opera singers advised a girl with great musical ability—but who lacked self-confidence and self-assertion—to stand before a mirror every day and, assuming a magnificent pose, say to herself, "I, I, I," with all the emphasis and power she could muster. He coupled this by telling her to simultaneously imagine that she was the then leading ballerina of the day. He told her that as she affirmed herself and constantly played the role, she would acquire the habit of self-confidence, which would be worth everything to her. "Assume your art boldly and fearlessly," he told her, "and hold yourself with a dignity and power corresponding with the character." This advice, which she followed literally, was worth more to this timid girl than scores of music lessons. The practice in it increased her confidence in herself wonderfully, and she was soon cured of her shyness and timidity.

The habit of *claiming as our own, as a vivid reality that which we desire*, has a tremendous magnetic power. There is a mysterious power in the spoken word, in the stalwart affirmation of a thought, which registers a profound impression on the subconscious mind—whereupon the silent forces within us proceed to make the word flesh, to make the thought we affirm a reality.

"But as the rain cometh down, and the snow from heaven, and returned not hither," says Isaiah, "but watered the earth and maketh it bring forth and bud, that it may give seed to the sower, and break to the eater: So shall my word be that goeth out of my mouth: it shall not return unto me void, but it shall accomplish that which I please, and it shall prosper *in the thing* whereto I sent it."

The constant vigorous assertion of "I am health; I am vigor; I am power; I am principle; I am truth; I am justice; I am beauty, because I am made in the image of perfection, of harmony, of truth, of justice, of immortal beauty"—tends to the manifestation of these things in our lives, to the degree we believe in what we are saying.

Great things are done under our repeated conviction of our ability to do whatever we undertake. But many of us seldom ever give thought to the words we utter, to the reality that our uttered thoughts are living forces and are made flesh. Yet those words are continually being manifest in our bodies, shaping our faces and expressions, and molding our destinies to their likeness.

Those immersed in material things and who live only to make money, for example, *believe* they will make it—*know* that they can make it; *affirm* that they will make it. They do not say to themselves every morning, "Well, I do not know whether I can make anything today. I will try. I may succeed and I may not." They simply and positively asserts that they can do what they desire—and then start out to put into operation plans and forces which will bring it about.

There is tremendous creative power in registering your vow; in the vigorous, determined affirmation; in the stout self-assertion; in the vigorous affirmation of the ego—of the "I," the "I am"—backed by a persistent, dogged endeavor to bring about the thing you desire. Those who have once properly put this technique into practice never again doubt its efficacy.

You must, however, *believe* what you affirm. If you affirm "I, am health; I am prosperity I am this or that," but do not believe it, you will not be helped by affirmation.

No matter whether you feel like it or not, just affirm that you *must* feel like it, that you *will* feel like it, that you *do* feel like it—that whether you are doing so now are not, you have it within your capacity to do your best. Speak your affirmation deliberately, affirm it vigorously, *and it will come true*.

Audible self-suggestion, which is simply a continuation or extension of the affirmation principle, is also one of the greatest aids to self-development. This talking to oneself vigorously; earnestly, arouses the sleeping forces in the subconscious self even more effectually than *thinking* about them.

There is a force in spoken words which is not stirred by going over the same words mentally. Words spoken aloud arouse slumbering energies within us which thinking does not stir up; when vocalized they make a more lasting impression on the mind—just as we are so much more impressed and inspired by listening to a great lecture or sermon than we would be if we read the same words in print; or how *seeing* things in nature makes a more lasting impression upon the mind than *thinking* about them. A vividness, a certain force, accompanies the spoken word—especially if earnestly, vehemently uttered—which is not conveyed in merely thinking about what words express. If you repeat to yourself aloud, vigorously, even vehemently, a firm resolve, you are more likely to carry it to reality than if you merely resolve in silence.

We can talk to our inner or other self, just as we would talk to a child; and we know from experience that it will listen to and act on our suggestions. We are, after all, constantly sending suggestions or commands to this inner self. We may not do so audibly, but we do so silently, mentally. Unconsciously, we advise, we suggest, we try to influence it in certain directions.

Many people have killed character enemies, peace and happiness enemies, have doubled and quadrupled their self-confidence, have strengthened tremendously their initiative, their executive ability—have literally made themselves over by talks with themselves and self-affirmations.

A remarkably successful friend of mine says that he has been wonderfully helped by talking to himself about his faults and shortcomings. "Heart-to-heart talks" with himself he calls these little exhortations. If he thinks his ambition is lagging, he gives himself a mental exercise which tends to sharpen and improve it. If he thinks his standards are lowering, he braces up his ideal by perpetually affirming his ability to do better and to climb higher everyday. It does not matter what the fault is—dawdling, being late in keeping appointments, losing his temper, being fractious and unreasonable with his employees—whatever it may be, he talks himself out of it. In his talks, he calls himself by name, and carries a picture of his other, better, diviner self in his mind; persistently holding before himself the image of the man he wants to be longs to be, and constantly affirms his ability to be. He says that nothing else has done half as much for him as this habit of talking things over with himself.

He says that he starts out every morning with the determination that he is going to be a bigger man at night than he was in the morning; that he is going to stand for more; that he is going to carry more weight in his community. He talks to himself about his failures of the day before and about his program for the day, while he is dressing in the morning, something after this fashion:

> "Now, John, you lost your temper yesterday; you went all to pieces over a mistake that some one made in the office; you made; a fool of yourself, so that your employees thought less of you than before, and it totally unfitted your mind for doing the large things that were clamoring for your attention. Don't make that mistake today. You are a pretty small man if you cannot rise above the petty details which confuse and block shallow minds. If you cannot rise above the trivial details of your office you are not a leader."

One of his greatest weaknesses was that of indecision. He had a perfect horror of settling an important thing so that it could not be reopened for consideration. He would always leave things until the last minute—his letters unsealed, papers unsigned, contracts open—until he was actually forced to close them, for fear he might want to reconsider his decisions.

He tells me that he finally overcame this weakness by constantly telling himself how foolish it was; how this vacillating habit would handicap his whole career, and how all people of executive ability—those who do great things—are characterized by their quick, strong decisions.

Another young man, who lives in New York, recently told me that he tries to walk through Central Park every morning on his way to business in order to get a chance to talk to himself alone. During these talks, he tells himself that, let what will come during the day, he must not lose his self-control; he must be a gentleman under all circumstances; that he must not allow worry, anxiety, or unfortunate moods to waste his energy, but must work it all up into effectiveness.

He says that this self "jacking-up"—as he calls it—this self-tuning in the morning, not only helps him to get a larger efficiency into his day's work, but also to do the work with much less wear and tear. It is a tremendous tonic. It stimulates him to better and better work. Since he has adopted the self-communing, self-bracing habit, he has gone ahead by leaps and bounds.

We would all be helped by the habit of talking to ourselves just as though we were another person in whom we were very much interested and to whom we were going to give our best advice. Talk to yourself as you would to some friend whom you love; someone who you know has ability but lacks courage and pluck. Reinforce yourself; reinvigorate your mind; reassure yourself.

Get so far away from others that you will not be conscious of their presence, and then go through your resolutions verbally—with vehemence, if necessary. You will soon be surprised to find how much better they will stick in your consciousness, and how much more likely you are to follow your own advice when you give it orally.

If you have some habit which is keeping you back, sapping the life out of you, you will be greatly strengthened in your power to overcome it by constantly saying to yourself,

> "I know this thing (calling it by name) is destroying my vitality. I am not so vigorous; so robust physically and mentally; I am not so efficient, as I should be; I do not think so clearly, I cannot control my mind so well as I could were I not hampered by this weakness. "The paralyzing habit is placing me at a great disadvantage in life; it is holding me up to ridicule, to unfavorable comparison with others. I know that I have more ability than many of those about me who are accomplishing a great deal more. Now, I am going to conquer this thing which is destroying my prospects and happiness. I am going to get freedom for myself at any cost."

Just talk to yourself in this way, whenever alone and you will be surprised to see how quickly the audible suggestion will weaken the grip of the vicious habit. In a short time your self-talks will so strengthen your will power that you will be able to entirely eradicate your weakness.

But you must be very positive in the affirmation of your ability to overcome it. If you simply say to yourself, "I know that this thing is bad for me; I know that if I continue to drink, or to smoke cigarettes, or to practice immorality, it will interfere with my success, but I do not believe I shall ever be able to overcome it; it has gotten such a hold on me that I cannot give it up"—you will never make any headway.

People who affirm by saying that "If God willing," or "If Providence so wills" they will then do this or that, little realize how the doubt expressed by the "if" takes the edge from their positiveness, and tends to produce negative minds.

The intensity of your affirmation of your confidence in your ability to do what you attempt is definitely and directly related to the degree of your achievement. To confront life's vicissitudes, we often need great projectile-power: It is easier to force a huge shell through the steel plates of a ship when projected with lightning speed from a cannon than to try to push it through slowly.

Stoutly, constantly, everlastingly affirm that you will become what your ambitions indicate as fitting and possible. Do not say "I shall be a success sometime," say, "I *am* a success. Success is my birthright" Do not say that you are going to be happy *in the future*. Say to yourself, "I was intended for happiness, made for it, and I am happy."

Always stoutly affirm your ability to conquer.

Don't be disappointed if you do not get immediate relief. Continue to talk to yourself in a confident manner, especially upon retiring, always affirming your ability to overcome your weakness, whatever it may be, and you will conquer it. Your will power will assist you, but conviction is a thousand times stronger than will power, and the constant affirmation of the ability of the power within you to overcome the thing which handicaps you will finally help you to conquer.

At first it may seem silly to you to be talking to yourself. Never mind. You will find that in time you will increase your confidence in yourself by the affirmation of what you are determined to be and to do, and in proportion, your ability to do it will increase.

No matter what other people may think or say about you, never allow yourself to doubt that you can do what you will to do. Boldly, confidently assert that there is a special place for you in the world, an individual role which only you can fill, and that you are going to fill it. Train yourself to expect great things of yourself. Never admit, even by your manner, that you think you are destined to do little things all your life Soon, you will derive so much benefit from your self-affirmations that you will have recourse to them in remedying all your defects—as there is no shortcoming, no obstacle to your happiness, however great or small, which will not succumb to persistent audible suggestion.

For example, you may be naturally timid and shrink from meeting people; and you may distrust your own ability. If so, you will be greatly helped by assuring yourself in your daily self-talks that you are not timid; that, on the contrary, you are the embodiment of courage and bravery. Assure yourself that there is no reason why you should be timid, because there is nothing inferior or peculiar about you; that you are attractive, and that you know how to act in the presence of others. Say to yourself that you are never again going to allow yourself to harbor any thoughts of self-depreciation or timidity or inferiority; that you are going to hold your head up and go about as though you were a king, a conqueror, instead of crawling about like a whipped cur. You are going to assert your selfhood, your individuality.

If you lack initiative, stoutly affirm your ability to begin things, and to push them through to a finish. If you will be sincere with yourself and strong and persistent in your affirmations, you will be surprised to see how you can increase your courage, your confidence, and your ability to execute your ideas.

Never worry that you are being watched or laughed at if you have these heart-to-heart talks with yourself publicly. If you suffer from self-consciousness or oversensitiveness, think of yourself as a king or a queen. Say to yourself constantly: "I am a king (or queen). There is no reason why I should consider myself inferior to others. I will just walk about as though I were governor of my state, or mayor of my city, entitled to do walk this land—master of the situation."

I know a young man who was so self-conscious when a youth that he would cross the street to avoid meeting anyone he knew. He was completely confused when anyone he was not accustomed to see chanced to speak to him. He was constantly depreciating himself and belittling his ability. Indeed, I have rarely seen any one who depreciated a splendid ability so much as he did. Yet he has so entirely overcome these faults by audible suggestion that no one would suspect that he had ever lacked self-appreciation or confidence, or that he had been a victim of shyness.

He tells me that he used to go out in the country and talk to himself seriously about his failings. "Now, Arthur, either there is something in you or there is not; and. I am going to find out," he would say. "Do not be a fool. You are just as good as anybody else, so long as you behave as well. Hold up, your head and be a man. Do not be afraid to face anybody. Go about among people as though you were somebody. Quit his everlasting self-depreciation, self-effacement. You are God's child, and you have just as good a right on this glad green earth as anybody else. Do not go about apologizing for being alive, or imagining you are taking up room which belongs to others."

He says that he also derives very great benefit from praising and appreciating himself audibly when he has done unusually well, or has acquitted himself as a man. On such occasions he will say: "Arthur, that was fine! You did splendidly! I am proud of you. That just shows what you are capable of. Do as well in every instance, and you will amount to something in the world and be somebody." You will find a wonderful advantage in starting out every morning with the mind set toward success and achievement by permeating it with thoughts of prosperity and harmony. It will then be so much the harder for discord to get into the day's work. If you are inclined to doubt your ability to do a particular thing, school yourself to hold the self-trust though firmly and persistently. It is the assumption of power, of self-trust, of confidence in yourself, in your integrity or wholeness, that cannot be shaken, that will enable you to *become* strong, to do, with vigor and east, the thin you undertake.

You will find that the perpetual hold of these ideal will change your whole outlook upon life. You will approach your problems from a new standpoint, and life will take on a fresh meaning. This perpetual affirmation will put you in harmony with your surroundings; it will make you contented and happy; and it will be a powerful tonic for your health. It will help you to build up individuality and personal power.

The objective side of us has a wonderful power to inspire and to encourage the subjective side—to arouse the subconscious mentality where all latent power and possibilities lie; to read to the deep within us where dwells slumbering powers, powers that would astonish us, that we never dreamed of possessing; forces that would revolutionize our lives if aroused and put into action.

The majority of us call out but a very small percentage of these latent forces which are waiting to serve us. Some pass the half-century mark before some emergency or crisis in their lives lifts the lid off their possibilities, many go through life without ever getting a glimpse of their powers.

The trouble is that we do not make a loud enough call upon the Great Within of us, our higher, more potent selves. We are too timid, too tame in our demands.

If you are not satisfied with your progress so far, if you are not growing bigger and broader in character, more efficient in your work, then something is holding you back, hindering you from making your ideal real. Find out what it is and then remove it by audible self-treatments. Affirm that which you wish, and it will be manifest in your life. Affirm it confidently, with the utmost faith, without any doubt of what you affirm.

Look into your own soul and take an account of your personal stock, your success and failure qualities. Analyze yourself as you would a friend you were eager to help, and whose strong and weak points you could see clearly. Then assert your possession of the things you need; of the qualities you long to own. Force your mind toward your goal; hold it there steadily, persistently, for this is the mental condition that creates. The negative mind, which doubts and wavers, creates nothing.

And always put your resolve into action at the first opportunity.

It is of the utmost importance to keep in mind, in other words, that it is the spiritual life that does the healing through words. Just as, therefore, faith without the spirit of good works is of no avail, words without life behind them are cold and ineffectual.

When you long for a thing that is right for you to have, affirm in perfect confidence that the thing is already yours. Claim it as a reality. Then do what you can on the material plane to make it yours. Soon you will reap what you have sown in thought and in positive affirmation.

Remember, though, that it is the life, the driving power of the spirit, that gives the word its power. If you don't mean what you say, if you don't live the meaning into your words, they are mere idle breath. You might just as well be saying "I'm a successful play-wright," yet not even be writing a play; or having written one, leave it in your desk drawer.

When you set your mind toward achievement, let everything about you indicate success. Let your manner, your dress, your bearing, your conversation, and everything you do speak achievement and success. Carry always a success atmosphere with you.

"I, myself, am good fortune," says Walt Whitman.

If we could, through the practice of constant self-affirmation, only realize that the very attitude of assuming that we *are* the embodiment of the thing we long to be or to attain, that we need not aspire to the good things we long for but that we *are* these qualities, we could then say with Pistol in *The Merry Wives of Windsor*, "Why then, the world's mine oyster."

And the happiness we so often desperately struggle to obtain would easily and daily be ours.

Today I will…

- *Begin having more frequent heart-to-heart talks with myself. By doing so, you can change your whole nature, revolutionize your career.*

- *Take notice of the moments in my day in which I experienced happiness, joy, pleasure, etc., and affirm my right to those sorts of moments and more like them.*

- *Write out a list of the qualities of a strong, courageous, successful character. Call them off aloud—"faith," "courage," "self-confidence," "ambition," enthusiasm," perseverance," "concentration," initiative," "cheerfulness," optimism," thoroughness," etc. Ask yourself if you possess these splendid qualities, or if you incline to their opposites. Don't be afraid to face your weak points, to call them by their right names. Bring them into the light, see them for what they are—to grapple with them. Ask yourself what you can do to improve them. Examine what you can do to add even more luster and expression to your strong points.*

When you have done that, go over the specific character qualities and ask yourself these broader questions; always visualizing and addressing yourself by name:

"What am I, _____ (your name here and in the blanks in the following questions) here for? What do you, _____, mean to the world? What message does my life, my career, bring to it? What do I _____ mean to my community? What do I _____ stand for? What do you _____ represent? Do you realize that you _____ were sent here with a message for humanity? Are you delivering it—patiently, persistently, determinedly, without grumbling, whining or shirking? What are you _____ giving to the world? Do I _____ mean much of anything to anybody but yourself? Is my sole aim to get more reputation, more money, more comforts for yourself? Does your pursuit of your ambition shut others out of your life? Are you _____ dreaming of the big thing you are going to do tomorrow, or are you doing the little things which you can do today; giving yourself as you go along; giving, if you have nothing else to give, encouragement, inspiration, helpfulness to those on the way with you? Would your community miss you _____ very much you should drop out of it?"

Probe yourself in this manner until you get a good line on yourself, a fair estimate of yourself; until you know both your strength and your weakness; until you can see with clear eyes the things that are keeping you back, the lack in your nature that is handicapping you, the weakness that is cutting down the average of your ability by ten, twenty, fifty or even seventy-five per cent. Then vigorously attack your enemies— the enemies of your success, of your efficiency, of your happiness. Daily and repeatedly stoutly affirm your complete mastery over them, their powerlessness to dominate your life and ruin your career and happiness.

→ *Create a list of affirmations for yourself. Affirmations are affirmative statements about you. They are always in the present tense ("I am…."), always positive ("I am…," rather than "I am not"), can be visualized, carry a strong emotional tone, and affirm a quality, characteristic, trait about yourself. It may be a quality, characteristic, or trait that you don't display very often or at all in your life right now. Don't let that inhibit you. There was at time when you didn't have the traits that you now find undesirable about yourself. You acquired them by others affirming them about you and you eventually accepting them ("I guess I really am not very talented, pretty, sexy, etc, etc."). Now, in a similar manner, you can affirm the traits you desire, and in equal like manner, in time, you will erase the old and acquire the new.*

→ *The following strong, positive affirmations—by C.D. Larson—are very suggestive and would make a splendid daily exercise:*

"I daily become more than I am."

"I achieve more because I know that I can."

"I recognize only that which is good in myself; that which is good in others."

"I am more determine when adversity threatens than ever in my life to prove that I can turn all things to good account."

"I wish only for that which can give freedom and truth, which can add to the welfare of the earth and all who live on it."

"I always speak to give encouragement, inspiration, and joy."

"I work to be of service to an ever-increasing number; my ruling desire shall be to enrich, ennoble, and beautify existence for all who may come my way."

Remember to speak these affirmations with feeling, conviction, and to see yourself—visualize yourself—

experiencing the things you are speaking.

[Many people have trouble with "I am," "I do," I always" affirmations—in a word, "I"-statements. They feel that they're uttering something untrue, as when a person who has difficulty controlling his or her spending says "I am now practicing prudent and effective spending habits." Their critical faculties chime in with "Oh no you're not!" One way to quiet that critical voice is to change "I am now practicing…." to "I can practice…." The critical mind is less apt to interrupt the latter, because intellectually there's nothing that says that even though you're not now practicing prudent and effective spending habits (or whatever it is you're affirming), you can't. And while "I can" may seem to be expressing some future rather than present action, if you examine it carefully, you'll see that it is an expression about you in your present state. (You could also say "It's okay to….") Another way to quiet the critical voice is to express your affirmations this way: "How wonderfully satisfying (fulfilling, whatever) it is to me to practice prudent and effective spending habits." Here again, your critical mind can't argue with that, because whether you're currently practicing sound spending habits, it's still nonetheless true that doing so—even just the thought of doing so—is satisfying for you.]

➔ _____
_____
➔ _____
_____
➔ _____
_____
➔ _____
_____

chapter 4

SELF-CONTROL

I will be lord over myself. —Goethe

He that would govern others first should be the master of himself.
—Massinger

Keep cool, and you command everybody. —St. Just

Real glory springs from the conquest of ourselves; and without that, the
conqueror is naught but the veriest slave. —Thomson

Strength of character consists of two things—
power of will and power of self-restraint.
It requires two things, therefore, for its existence—
strong feelings and strong command over them.
—F. W. Robertson

Do you think," asked Mrs. Rasper, "that a little temper is a bad thing in a woman?" "Certainly not," replied her husband; "it is a good thing, and she ought never to lose it."

Mrs. Livingstone, the mother of the missionary, and Mrs. Byron, the mother of the poet, had each put into their hands one of nature's finest gems: the calm Christian temper of the one preserved her gem for a life of almost unqualified nobility; the uncontrolled temper of the other made hers little better than a splendid ruin.

No one has a temper naturally so good that it does not need attention and control; and none a temper so bad but that, by proper culture, it may become pleasant.

The celebrated Mr. Fletcher of Saltoun was possessed of a very irritable temper. His butler intimated his intention of seeking another place, but Mr. Fletcher proceeded gently to urge him to continue in his service.

"I cannot bear your temper, sir," said the butler.

"I am passionate, I confess," said, Mr. Fletcher, "but my passion is no sooner on than it is off."

"Yes," rejoined the butler, "but then it's no sooner off than it's on again!"

Dumont heard Mirabeau deliver a report on Marseilles; every word was interrupted by abusive epithets "calumniator, liar, assassin, scoundrel." Mirabeau paused, and, in honeyed tone, addressing the most furious, said, "I wait, Messieurs, till these amenities be exhausted."

I have heard," says Matthew Henry, "of a married couple, who, though both of a hasty temper, yet lived comfortably together by observing a rule on which they had agreed—never to be both angry at the same time."

"I am Apollyon," said a crank who invaded the library of the Duke of Wellington. "I am sent to kill you."

"Kill me? Very odd."

"I am Apollyon, and must put you to death."

"Obliged to do it today?"

"I am not told the day or the hour, but I must do my mission."

"Very inconvenient," said the duke, "very busy—great-many letters to write. Call again, and write me word—I'll be ready for you."

The duke went on with his correspondence. The maniac was appalled and calmed by the matter-of-fact coolness of the stern, immovable old man, and backed out of the room.

In the window of a room in Queen's College, Oxford, is an inscription which records that it was once occupied by the young hero king, Henry V., who is described as "VICTOR HOSTIUM ET SUI"—conqueror of his enemies and of himself. He conquered his enemies at Agincourt; but the conquest of himself required a far more desperate struggle.

Beaconsfield was asked how he managed to retain the favor of the queen. His answer was, "You see, I never contradict, and I sometimes forget." A good rule for others besides prime-ministers.

A nominee of his political party was directed to an experienced politician for lessons in political success and the way to gain votes. The elder gave set out terms, adding, "Five dollars for every time you break my directions."

"All right," said the nominee.

"When will you begin?" asked the instructor.

"Right off, this moment."

"Very well. The first lesson is, *you must never resent any evil you hear of yourself.* Be on your guard all the time."

"Oh, that I can do. I can brace up against what people say of me. I care nothing for that."

"Very well; that is the first of my lessons; though, after all, I must be frank to say that I don't want such an unprincipled rascal as you are elected."

"Sir, how dare you…."

"Five dollars, if you please."

"Oh! Ah! It's a lesson, is it?"

"Well, yes; it's a lesson. But then, I mean it all just the same."

"You impudent…."

"Five dollars, please."

"Oh! Ah!" he gasped. "Another lesson. That makes ten dollars so soon."

"Yes, ten dollars; would you mind paying as we go; for, unless you pay better than you have the name of paying your debts in general…."

"You infernal rascal!"

"Five dollars, please."

"Ah! Another lesson. Well, I would better try to keep my temper."

"Well, I'll take it all back; I didn't really mean it, of course. For I think you are a very respectable sort of man, considering what a low-lived family you come from, and what a disreputable man your father was."

"You infamous scoundrel!"

"Five dollars, please."

So went this first lesson in self-control, for which the aspiring political candidate paid so dearly. Then the elder politician made his point: "Now, instead of a five-dollar bill," he said, "bear in mind that you lose one vote, at least, every time you lose your temper or resent an insult, and that votes are worth more to you than bank-bills."

Nothing else makes such havoc in, the lives of ordinary men and women as yielding to sudden fits of anger. How sweet, on the other hand, the serenity of habitual self-command! How many stinging self-reproaches it spares us! If you are conscious of being in a passion, keep your mouth shut, lest you increase your passion. Many a person has dropped dead in a rage. Fits of anger bring fits of disease.

"Be calm in arguing," said George Herbert, "for fierceness makes error a fault, and truth discourtesy."

Socrates said that when he found in himself any disposition to anger, he would check it by speaking low.

"How do you keep out of quarrels?" asked a friend of another. "Oh, easily enough: If a man gets angry with me, I let him have the quarrel all to himself."

When do we feel more at ease with ourselves than when we have passed through a sudden and strong provocation *without speaking a word, or in undisturbed good humor*! When, on the contrary, do we feel a deeper humiliation than when we are conscious that anger has made us betray ourselves by word, look, or action? Nervous irritability is the greatest weakness of character. It is the sharp grit which aggravates friction, and cuts out the bearings of the entire human machine.

At Chester, Penn., lived a shopkeeper who was noted for his patience. One day a man determined to try it. He asked for this cloth and that, and in half a dozen kinds and colors. At last one seemed to suit him. "That's what I want. Now you may give me a cent's worth." The imperturbable shopkeeper took out a cent, cut a piece of cloth to cover it, did it up in a paper, and passed it to the discomfited customer.

John Henderson was debating with an Oxford student, when the latter grew angry, and threw a glass full of wine in his face. Henderson calmly wiped his face, and coolly said, "This, sir, is a digression; now for the argument."

Spies have exhibited self-control in the highest degree; a moment off guard, and they hang for it. One spy, when captured, pretended to be deaf and mute. The most ingenious devices were resorted to, but he kept deaf and mute. At last his captors said, "Well, you can go," but he did not show by the slightest sign that he knew the ordeal was over. They said, "He is what he pretends to be, or a fool." His perfect self-control saved his neck.

Professor Blaikie once put the notice on his recitation-room door, "Will meet the Classes tomorrow." A wag erased the "C," making the notice read, "Will meet the lasses tomorrow." The professor, happening to pass by the room before he left town, saw, smiled, and erased the "l," leaving the note to now read, "Will meet the asses tomorrow." His self-control and ready wit won him over further to his students.

Donald McCrie was a Scot, whose canniness once stood him in good stead. Down in the country he kept a small grocery and variety store, with dim windows, dusty cobwebs, and slow sales. He sent up to London for "forty pons" (pounds) of indigo, replenishment to last a dozen years. The order was misread; but what was known of Donald was favorable, and his supposed order was honored, and the invoice of forty tons was sent.

Amazement possessed poor Donald. For a week he went about as if dazed, but kept his counsel. He thought of all the ways indigo could be used—but forty tons! Yet he kept still. Down came a spruce drummer from the metropolis, with coach and span, found Donald in his close quarters, glibly told him that the London firm was convinced there was a mistake, and that he had come to rectify it, and take back the consignment, and would generously pay the freight.

The firm would not send a man in this style for nothing, thought Donald, and so he did not admit that there had been a mistake.

The agent then said, "Come over to the public house."

But Donald controlled his love for the good wine, thinking, Now is the time for a clear head.

By every means the agent tried to make him talk; but Donald parried, and said that "he must not suppose a Scotchman would act without knowing what he was doing." The clerk lost his self-control, and said, "The fact is, we have had a call for more indigo than we had by us, and we will pay you a bonus of five hundred pounds, and the freight."

Donald shook his head; his thought was that he must see the length of that rope. Another offer was refused; at last the clerk pulled out his instructions and said: "Here, obstinate man, that is as far as I can go—five thousand pounds."

Donald calmly accepted. The crop had failed in the West Indies, and government troops had to have blue for their army coats. Donald McCrie made a fortune by his self-control.

The absence of profanity in one's speech is also a sign of self-control. Profanity never did any man the least good. It is a sign of weakness. No one is richer, happier, or wiser for it. It recommends no one to society; it is disgusting to refined people, and abominable to the good.

"My lads," said a naval captain, when reading his orders to the crew on the quarterdeck to take command of the ship, "there is a favor which I ask of you, and which; as a British officer, I expect will be granted by a crew of British seamen. What say you, my lads? Are you willing to grant your new free mind, and captain, who promises to treat you well, one favor?"

"Hi, hi, sir," cried all hands. "Please to let's know what it is, sir." "Why, my lads," said the captain, "it is this: that *you must allow me to use the first oath on this ship.*"

Those without self-control, however great their abilities, are always at the mercy of their moods and circumstances. They cannot fling himself against the enemy.

Clarendon said of the great Hampden "He was supreme governor over his passions, and he had thereby great power over other men's."

Perfect self-control means such thorough mastery over self as Robert Ainsworth, the lexicographer, possessed, who, when his wife, in a fit of passion, committed his voluminous manuscript to th flames, calmly turned to his desk and recommenced his labors.

We measure a person by the strength the power of the feelings he or she subdues, not by the power of those which subdue him or her.

We need our passions, they are the winds which urge our vessel forward. Reason is the pilot which steers it. Our vessel could not advance without the winds, and without the pilot it would be lost. The truly successful people, however, have both faculties under self-control. Such people have a strong grip upon themselves and hold themselves to their tasks—under good fortune and bad, through prosperity and adversity.

Self-control gives confidence, not only in the possessor, but in others. Self-control gives credit in the business place. Banks are inclined to trust those who can control themselves, as they offer the promise of being more reliable. Employers know that employees who cannot control themselves will similarly be neither able to control neither their own nor others' affairs.

Self-control will succeed with one talent, while self-indulgence will fail with ten. You may succeed without education and without health, but you cannot succeed without self-control—that mighty grip upon yourself which enables you to march through opposition and misfortune and into a life of self-approval.

A self-controlled mind is a free mind, and freedom is power.

And contentment.

And happiness.

Today I will...

→ *Reevaluate my tendency to want to get in the last word. We often feel wronged and persist in attempting to get the other person to see the error of his or her ways and the rightness of ours. Sometimes this is appropriate, but often it only escalates our feeling of stress. Determine what fights you truly must fight, and what battles you can walk away from. In some situations, it might be better to let the other person win—it might turn out to be a lesser victory than your not getting into a shouting match.*

→ *Let a kind word become more easily spoken than an unkind one. It is easy to get lured into unkind gossip; it is often very difficult to avoid it: one risks being censured by one's colleagues if one doesn't join in in the gossip. But at the end of the day, your conscience will invariably trouble you and happiness will elude you, if you don't practice the wisdom of "If you've not got anything good to say, then don't say anything."*

→ *Practice calmness in the midst of chaos, hostility, anger, and the like. In the midst of bedlam, it is often the calm person who is most admired and sought out. And it's always the one who has nothing to apologize for.*

→ *Remind myself that if I'm in a situation in which I feel that my temper is going to get the better of me, it's okay to walk away from the situation, promising to come back later. Too often we let our tempers, our hurt feelings run away with us, and we say or do things we later regret—pushing happiness that much further from us. Even if it turns out that we are right, we may still regret not what we said, but how we said it. It's okay, therefore, to tell someone, "I'm getting very angry right now, and that's not a good time for me to try to express myself. I'm going to go outside (sit down, go for a drive, whatever) and calm myself, take a new look at this situation, and then I promise you that I'll come back and talk with you." Remember that having the wherewithal to step away is important, but so too is making,* and keeping, *the promise to resume talking at a later time (and where appropriate, specify the time, e.g., "I'll be back in an hour"; "I'll talk with you about this again tomorrow"; etc.)*

→ _____
  _____
→ _____
  _____
→ _____
  _____
→ _____
  _____

chapter 5

RICHES AND HAPPINESS

The world is too much with us; late and soon,
Getting and spending, we lay waste our powers:
Little we see in Nature that is ours;
We have given our hearts away, a sordid boon!
—Wordsworth

The power of material things to bestow happiness, to bring joy into life, is tremendously exaggerated. And, indeed, what a misfortune it would be if wealth were in truth the singular source of happiness, as so many people think it is: The wealthy would always be happy and the poor would always be unhappy. Fortunately, riches alone do not make people happy or blessed. Indeed, one of the greatest disappointments of many of the rich is their discovery that they have not been able to purchase happiness with money; that what money can buy only satisfies a small part of an immortal being.

"Money never yet made a man happy," said Benjamin Franklin "and there is nothing in its nature to produce happiness."

Yet, despite such cautions, despite some of the richest and happiest minds having belonged to people who had very little of this world's goods, the great struggle of the thousands is still to acquire riches as a means of obtaining happiness. What those others had was a wealth which no money could buy, no envy purchase. And yet, instead of envying *them*, most of us envy those with great sums of wealth.

Why should the sight of other people's prosperity kill my appreciation and enjoyment of my possessions? Why should I enjoy mine less because somebody else has more? Why, though, should the fact that other people have more than I, take the value out of what I have? Why should I depreciate myself and bow and scrape to the people who have managed to rake together a huge pile of dollars. Is the dollar the measure of the things that are worthwhile? Is the dollar pile greater than the person? If it is happiness we seek, there must be something finer and richer and infinitely greater inside of us than the ideal of how much material things we can pile up about ourselves.

Indeed, the pursuit of wealth alone brings a great many enemies with it, enemies which tempt us to do a great many things which are not for our best interest and which deteriorate our souls and vitiate our characters. Many of the rich, for example, are conspicuously noted for the absence of their names from among those connected with all worthy objects—who seldom give to the poor, who never lend a hand to worthy causes, who belong to no organizations whose object is to help humanity. To be that rich in money and that poverty-stricken in everything else is not to be rich, but to be poor.

If we concentrate upon greed, if our mental attitude is always fixed upon the moneymaking game and our own self-interests, then there is nothing in our thoughts to make happiness ours. Moreover, what began as a habit develops into an addiction, and when someone becomes addicted, he or she loses a sense of moral obligation, loses an appreciation of truth and of duty, developing only a marvelous cunning for procuring that which will satisfy his or her craving. In that environment, it becomes impossible for those things which create love to live. Our base propensities kill the more tender plants and flowers within us, which radiate sweetness and beauty, contentment and happiness.

Wealth brings many new obligations, often accompanied by added complications. Instead of filling a vacuum, it often makes one. Robert Louis Stevenson appreciated the great impediment of material things to one's soul-flight heavenward. He once telegraphed his congratulations to a friend whose great and impressive house was burned down. Stevenson understood that while many think that they would be perfectly happy if only they could get money enough so that they could have the freedom to gratify all their desires, upon attainment of their fortunes, they would discover that money often brings thorns to torment its possessor. In this particular instance,

Stevenson's friend's wife was being driven to distraction with an army of servants and with the management of the great establishment.

One of the worst doctrines ever set forth is that real happiness is gained through material things. It is not. Real happiness is not a measure of the quantity of one's wealth or possessions, but of the quality of one's heart and mind. A great bank account can never make a person rich in happiness. It is the mind that makes the body rich. No one is rich in happiness, no matter how much money or land he or she may possess, who is poor in heart.

A wealthy man, when asked what deed of his life had given him the greatest happiness, replied that it was paying off a mortgage a poor woman's home which was being sold out from over her head. In helping to save the home of a poor woman, he had gained greater joy and satisfaction than in any experience of his business career.

The most unhappy people I know build their own purgatory by their false ideas of life, by putting the wrong emphasis on things, by setting the wrong value on things.

Recently, an employee told me the following story:

"I am only an ordinary mechanic and my employer talks as though I were a failure in life because I am not in business for myself, and haven't got rich. He tells me that *anybody* with an ounce of brains and pluck ought to be able to make a fortune in this land of opportunity.

"He and I have different ways of estimating what stands for success and happiness in life. He looks down upon me, regards me as a nobody, because I cannot live in as fashionable a part of the city as he does, nor afford an automobile. My family do not dress as his family dresses. My children cannot associate with the same people. We do not belong to his social set. I am not invited to go on committees, on boards of directors, as this man is. And yet, the truth be known, I have a better standing in the estimation of my neighbors than my employer. He is looked upon as a shrewd, cunning, long-headed schemer. People look up to his money, but not to him. They bow and scrape to his fortune.

"I began to work for Mr. B. as a boy on three dollars a week. It wasn't many years before I worked up to a master mechanic's position. I believe I have a greater respect for my occupation than he has for his. A beautiful piece of work, a well-done job, delights me as a superb painting delights an artist. But my employer seems to look upon his business merely as the most practicable means of piling up money."

To be so engulfed in one's occupation as this mechanic's employer, to be swallowed up in a complicated life, harassed by the striving and straining, the worry and anxiety which accompany busyness, is not to be either truly rich or happy. Yes, it is true, that if we eliminate everything in ourselves that aspires for the good, the beautiful, and the true; if we eliminate everything but the brute part of ourselves; then we are able to experience the brute's enjoyment—but we will never know that happiness that is available to us as human beings.

The greatest aim of our lives should be to absorb into our being the largest amount of sweetness and beauty it is capable of absorbing. It is not the possession of money that constitutes wealth, that gives the highest satisfaction and awakens the consciousness of noble achievement, or that gives the assurance that we are fulfilling our mission and that we are reading aright the sealed message which the Creator placed in our hands at birth. The highest riches are beyond the reach of money, are independent of fortune, and cannot be lost amidst the fluctuations of life. Happiness can no more be bought than love or respect can be bought.

Only the allegiance to ennobling and unchanging principles can give permanent happiness; material things are ever changing, ever elusive; there is no permanency, no endurance in them. As Emerson said, "Nothing can bring you peace but the triumph of principles." "Moderation in temper is always a virtue," said Thomas Paine, "but moderation in principle is always a vice." No one can be really happy who does not have a high ideal and a grand life purpose.

Pursuit of money wealth is more often than not an enemy of both principles and the simple life, creating instead a complicated, stressful, straining life—and we human beings are so constituted that a complex life is not conducive to our best well-being or our greatest happiness.

Time and again, I have traveled a long distance to visit a very humble home in Amesbury, Massachusetts. The whole property is worth but a few hundred dollars, but the fact that John Greenleaf Whittier lived there has given it an absolutely priceless value. Men and women cross continents and oceans to visit it. Enthusiastic admirers of the poet carry away from the spot bits of wood, wild flowers, leaves and all sorts of souvenirs to remind themselves that a man lived there—one of nature's noble men.

Thousands of people in this country look upon Whittier, the simple poet, as one of the richest treasures America has produced, and yet, considered from a commercial standpoint, all he left in the world was worth but a song.

And what is true of Whittier is true of many of the so-called poor, in whose homes and lives we often find more that inspires noble living, that lifts life above the commonplace and the sordid, and that stirs the soul to higher flights, than in the mansions of some of our millionaires, where we may find a display of wealth in rich carpets and tapestries, costly furniture and find furnishings—a fortune, in other words, in decorations—but nothing whatsoever to appeal to the spiritual qualities of life.

Who would insult the memory of Whittier by asking if he were rich? Who would desecrate the name of Lincoln by asking how much money he left?

And yet how many continue to believe that they can purchase happiness!

No one has yet been able to bribe real happiness. There is one price for happiness, and the poor may gain it as well as the rich.

It is folly to place such a tremendous emphasis upon money and what money will do. With money, we can, perhaps purchase momentary pleasures, but to set all of our life in pursuit of the dollar for such fleeting moments of reward is to mistake pleasure for happiness.

I do not mean to suggest that wealth and prosperity are wrong, that poverty is noble, or that all those who are wealthy have ignoble characters. But if it is happiness you seek, there must be some higher motive within you if you are to obtain lasting happiness. Money, to make people happy, must serve their higher nature—the development of the good in them and in others.

Only those who seek another's good, another's welfare, another's happiness, can find their own. With the sense of having done right, men and women have been known to be happy amid the most adverse circumstances. Without it, they are miserable, despite having every worldly want supplied.

Only soul wealth, generous disinterestedness, the love that seeks not its own, and hands that help and hearts that sympathize constitute true riches and fill the possessor with the joy of one who knows that he or she is fulfilling the real purpose of life.

The human heart will always be hungry. Unhappiness is the hunger to covet, to strive after, to get. Happiness, on the other hand, is the hunger to give. Happiness, in other words, was born a twin of hunger. To truly be happy, we must starve the one hunger and feed the other.

And yet everywhere we continue to see those who are starving their nobler growth in their restless strife to put a little more money into their purses. Multitudes have sacrificed family, homes, friendships, health, comforts, and honor itself, to appease that awful burning fever within, that terrible craving of the ambition for more, *more*—a perpetual hunger and thirst which are never satisfied but which instead chokes all their nobler aspirations, blighting all that is fine, delicate, and sensitive in their natures, until they become blunt and irresponsive to all that is beautiful, sweet, and true.

Is it not a pitiable sight to see a human being in the mad clutches of a greedy aim! Such a person is dead to all that is the best in life. He or she does not appreciate the glory and the grandeur, the sublimity, of existence.

Woe be to those who cater to an ambition of riches and follow it blindly, who expect it to give peace of mind when it is realized; for the more a greedily an ambition is fed, the more ravenous its appetite! It is like the firewater in the enchanted story; the more the victim drinks of it, the greater his or her burning fever.

To be truly happy there must be within each of us a hunger, an inclination, to help others and bring happiness into their lives; there must be within us an appreciation for *who we are* rather than *what we have*; there must be the capacity to appreciate to the utmost every situation in life These are what contribute to one's happiness. Those who have wealth without these higher purposes are soon led away from happiness.

If you do not incorporate these qualities into your life, if you to do not affirm them as the traits and principles necessary for your own enlargement and betterment, then true happiness will forever elude you, and you will never know the joy and satisfaction of true living—even though you may have millions of dollars.

Today I will...

- *Examine my priorities. Are you putting the acquisition of money ahead of the giving of your self? Do you cancel, postpone, time and affection for your family—asking them to understand that your job requires your time? Is that why you got married? Is that why you had a family?*
- *Ask myself if I am making a life or simply making a living. If latter, what can you do to change?*
- *Write out my most deeply held principles, and then see if I have compromised any of them for my work, in order to make money. If you have, what can you do to restore the balance, to reestablish the prominence of your cherished principles—those that make you feel worthwhile, rich in spirit not just in money—in your life?*
- *Look and see if I am using the money I earn to create happiness or to only satisfy a pleasure, a craving. In today's world of high-priced automobiles and high-priced technology, it is easy to believe that you must have the newest—the newest equipment, the newest machinery, etc.—when in truth what you currently have is serving you fine. Is the money you're spending on getting the newest, the debt you may be incurring, keeping you from going out to dinner, a concert, a play, having a picnic in a park, with your spouse? Your children? Or, if you are not yet married, is it keeping you from treating yourself to a concert, a play, a meal out, a movie, etc.?*
- *Set aside a portion of my income for tithing. There are many sources in life that give you spiritual happiness: the*

community symphony or dance group; the local non-commercial radio station; the church, the temple; the yoga center, the meditation center; etc. Each of these organizations has fund-raising drives or make periodic requests for financial assistance so they can continue providing you with that which nurtures you. Set aside a certain amount of money to give to these organizations. It doesn't have to be a lot. The giving is what will bring you happiness.

➔ _____
_____
➔ _____
_____
➔ _____
_____
➔ _____
_____

chapter 6

ENJOYING WITHOUT OWNING

Won't you come into the garden?
I would like my roses to see you.
　　—Richard B. Sheridan

Washington Irving told us of a French marquis, who consoled himself upon the loss of his chateau by remarking that he nonetheless still had available to him the gardens of Versailles. "When I walk through these fine gardens," the marquis said, "I have only to fancy myself the owner of them, and they are mine. All these gay crowds are my visitors, and I have not the trouble of entertaining them. My estate is a perfect *sans souci*, where every one does as he pleases, and no one troubles the owner. All Paris is my theater, and presents me with a continual spectacle. I have a table spread for me in every street, and thousands of waiters ready to fly at my bidding. When my servants have waited upon me, I pay them, discharge them, and there's an end. I have no fears of their wronging or pilfering me when my back is turned. Upon the whole," said the old gentleman with a smile of infinite good humor, "when I recollect all that I have suffered, and consider all I at present enjoy, I can but look upon myself as a person of singular good fortune."

The habit happiness, developed by the faculty of extracting beauty from everything you touch, is riches indeed. Why should we not feel rich in spirit in all that our eyes can carry away, no matter if others happen to have the title-deed? Why should I not enjoy the beautiful gardens of the wealthy and their grounds, just as if I owned them? As I pass by I can make the wealth of color my own. The beauty of plants, and lawn, and flowers, and trees are all mine. The title-deed of another does not cut off my aesthetic ownership.

The best part of the farm—the landscape, the beauty of the brook and the meadow, the slope of the valley, the song of the birds, the sunset—cannot be shut up within any title-deed; they belong to the eye that can carry them away, the mind that can appreciate them.

Did you ever realize how rich in joy you really are? You say you have no land, no home of your own; that you are only living in a small apartment?

Of what a lot of pleasure self-pity robs us!

We do not need to own in order to appreciate. We ought to be able to enjoy everything that is enjoyable, no matter who owns it. How foolish to envy others the things which we do not happen to have or cannot afford! Learn to enjoy what you cannot own. Be like the birds, who do not care who holds the title deed to the lands where, in their migrations, they joyously build their little homes.

Did you ever stop to think how small a part of the community really belongs to any individual? The streets, the roads, the parks, the public libraries, the rivers, the brooks, the mountains, the sunsets, the marvelous mysteries and beauties of the heavens are yours. Rockefeller cannot get more out of the sun than you can, or from the beauty of the moon. The stars and the change of the seasons are as much yours as his. The landscape belongs to you just as much as to the man who pays the taxes on the land.

Think of the fortune it costs a great city to keep up the parks! Even the estate of a Carnegie could not afford such grounds, and you are sure of always finding them in the finest condition without a thought of care from yourself or a bit of anxiety. The people who care for all these things are public servants, giving their service for you as much as for the richest. You do not have to hire them, watch them, or pay them. The flowers, the birds, the statuary, all of the beautiful things in our great parks, are as much yours as they are the property of the richest.

Robert Louis Stevenson once packed up his pictures and his furniture and sent them to an enemy who was about to be married. Then he wrote to a friend that he had at last rid himself of the master to whom he had been a bond slave. "Don't," he said, "give hostages to fortune, I implore you. Not once a month will you be in a mood to enjoy a picture. When that mood comes, go to the gallery and see it. Meanwhile let some hired flunky dust the picture and keep it in good condition for your coming."

Why should I scramble and struggle to get possession of a little portion of this earth? This is *my* world now, already. Why should I envy others its mere legal possession? Life belongs to those who can see it, enjoy it. I need not envy the so-called owners of estates around the world. They are merely taking care of my property and keeping it in excellent condition for me. For the price of gas, or bus, train, or airplane fare, I can, whenever I wish, see and possess the best of it all. And it has cost me no effort, it requires of me no care.

The green grass, the shrubbery, and the statues on the lawns of the great homes, the sculptures and the paintings within the great art museums, are always ready for me whenever I feel a desire to look upon them. I do not wish to carry them home with me, for I could not give them half the care they now receive. Besides, it would take too much of my valuable time, and I should be worrying continually lest they be spoiled or stolen. I have much of the wealth of the world now—and it is all prepared for me without any pains on my part! All the people around me are working hard to get things that will please me, and competing to see who can give them to me the cheapest.

Life and landscape are mine, the stars and flowers, the sea and air, the birds and trees. What more do I want? All the ages have been working for me; all mankind are my servants. I am only required to feed and clothe myself—an easy task in this land of opportunity.

Henry Ward Beecher used to say that it was a great treat to him to go out and enjoy the good things in the shop windows, especially during the Christmas holidays—and that he could look upon the architecture and sculpture of palatial homes as if his own, and enjoy the grounds no matter *who* had the title-deed to them.

Did you ever watch a bee flitting about from blossom to blossom? Can we not all, first-hand, draw in sustenance from the meadows, birds, brooks, mountains, and forest, just as the bee draws in honey from the flowers?

"Joys fall not to the rich alone," wrote Horace. We can all see the splendor in the flower, the glory in the grass, books in the running brooks, the sermons in stones, and the good in everything.

How is it, then, that some people find so much that enriches their lives, while others find so little? It is wholly a question of the quality of the appreciative heart. Some people are blind to beauty. They can travel with the utmost indifference in the midst of the most gorgeous and inspiring scenery. Their souls are not touched. They do not feel the inspiration which puts others into ecstasy.

"There are joys which long to be ours," a writer once wrote, "... which come about us like birds seeking inlet; but we are shut up to them, and so they bring us nothing, but sit and sing a while upon the roof and then fly away."

Be so constituted that you do not need to own things to enjoy them; that there is no envy in your nature. Then what you *will* own, will be happiness.

Today I will...

- *Not let myself miss out on the beauty around me just because I don't "own" it. Drive to the richest part of town. Let yourself appreciate that the beauty of the place—the lawns, the landscaping, the construction of the homes, the trees, the flower beds—knowing that it is as much yours to enjoy as those who own the properties ... and you don't have to pay the maintenance, the upkeep, the taxes, or work the long hours to "have" it. It's all there for you to enjoy and savor any day you want to go there. Then drive or walk home and thank the people who live in those homes for making and keeping that place beautiful for you to enjoy.*
- *Remind myself that nobody owns all the beauty in the world. Don't envy others for what beauty they are able to afford. Nobody owns all the castles in the world, all the mountain villas, all the beachfront or lakeside properties. Be thankful and appreciative that others have the means to make another*

spot on this earth beautiful, and that you can enjoy and "own" the beauty there as much as they.

→ *Go to one of the parks in my city if I am feeling discouraged, disheartened, overwhelmed, downtrodden, sorry for myself, and sit beside a pond, feed bread to the geese and ducks, or wander its trails, reminding myself that someone in my city has created this park and maintains this beauty, this opportunity of quietude and beauty, for me—so how poor can I be, how miserable, how sorry for myself?*

→ *Go to an art museum or art gallery in town. You don't have to purchase anything. If it is an art gallery you're in, just say "I'm just looking, thank you." Look at the works of art that others have created, and remind yourself that they have done so with the intent to enrich you, to bring you fulfillment. Nobody creates and displays without the hope that someone will enjoy. You can give them the gift of your enjoyment, and receive from them the gift of their wanting to give you enjoyment. It is something that you can give them and they you without your ever having to own the work of art. Indeed, the artist himself or herself did not intend appreciation to be limited to just the person who "owns." "Beauty is in the eye of the beholder," it is written—not the eye of the "owner." Today, behold!*

→ _____
_____
→ _____
_____
→ _____
_____
→ _____
_____

chapter 7

GIVING

"It is more blessed to give than to receive."
—Acts 20:35

Dining one day with Baron James Rothschild, Eugene Delacroix, the famous French artist, confessed that, during some time past, he had vainly sought for a head to serve as a model for that of a beggar in a picture which he was painting; and that, as he gazed at his host's features, the idea suddenly occurred to him that the very head he desired was before him. Rothschild, being a great lover of art, readily consented to sit as the beggar. The next day, at the studio, Delacroix placed a tunic around the baron's shoulders, put a stout stick in his hand, and made him pose as if he were resting on the steps of an ancient Roman temple. In this attitude he was found by one of the artist's favorite pupils, in a brief absence of the master from the room. The youth naturally concluded that the beggar had just been brought in, and with a sympathetic look quietly slipped a piece of money into his hand. Rothschild thanked him simply, pocketed the money, and the student left the room. Rothschild then inquired of the master, and found that the young man had talent, but very slender means. Soon after, the, youth received a letter stating that charity bears interest, and that the accumulated interest on the amount he had given to one he supposed to be a beggar was represented by the sum of ten thousand francs, which was awaiting his claim at the Rothschild office.

None of us is so poor as to not be able to give something to enrich another, every day of our lives.

"The most delicate, the most sensible of all pleasures," says LaBuyere, "consists in promoting the pleasures of others."

Hawthorne has said that the inward pleasure of imparting pleasure is the choicest of all.

And, said Carlyle, "There is no greatness [than] to make some nook of God's creation more fruitful, better, more worthy of God; to make some human heart a little wiser, happier, more blessed, less accursed!"

The gladness of having had some honorable share in the world's work, what is better than this?

To extend to all the cup of joy is indeed angelic business, and there is nothing that makes one more beautiful than to be engaged in it.

"The high desire that others may be blest savors of heaven."

The memory of those who spend their days in hanging sweet pictures of faith and trust in the galleries of sunless lives shall never perish from the earth.

To do good with money makes life a delight to the giver. How happy, then, was the life of Jean Ingelow, since what she received from the sale of a hundred thousand copies of her poems, and fifty thousand of her prose works, she spent largely in charity; one unique charity being a "copyright" dinner three times a week to twelve poor persons just discharged from the neighboring hospitals! Nor was any one made happier by it than the poet.

John Ruskin inherited a million dollars. "With this money he set about doing good," says a writer in the *Arena*. "Poor young men and women who were struggling to get an education were helped, homes for working men and women were established, and model apartment houses were erected. He also promoted a work for reclaiming waste land outside of London."

Ruskin was also ever liberal in aiding poor artists, and did much to encourage artistic taste among the young. On one occasion he purchased ten fine water-color paintings by Holman Hunt for $3,750, to be hung in the public schools of London. By 1877 he had disposed of three-fourths of his inheritance, besides all the income from his books. But the calls of the poor, and his plans of educating and ennobling the lives of working men, giving more sunshine and joy, were such that he determined to dispose of all the remainder of his wealth except a sum sufficient to yield him £1,500 a year on which to live.

If you have the blues, take a map and census table of the world and estimate how many millions there are who would gladly exchange lots with you. Then begin upon some practicable plan to do all the good you can to as many as you can, and you will forget to be despondent.

Charles George Gordon, known as "Chinese Gordon," after serving faithfully and valiantly in the great Chinese rebellion, and receiving the highest honors of the Chinese Empire, returned to England, caring little for the praise thus heaped on him. He settled at Gravesend, where he filled his house with boys from the streets, whom he taught and made men of, and then secured them places on ships—following them all over the world with letters of advice and encouragement.

Those who get the most out of life do the most to elevate others.

How happy were those Little Sisters of the Poor at Tours, who took scissors to divide their last remnant of bed clothing with an old woman who came to them at night, craving hospitality!

And how happy was that American school teacher who, during the late war, gave up the best room in the house at a mountain sanatorium, which she had engaged long before the season opened, taking instead the poorest room in the house, that, she might give good quarters to a soldier just out of his camp hospital!

How many of us are there, ready to make some great sacrifice, who neglect the little acts of kindness which make so many lives brighter and happier? The one great thing in life is to do a little good to everyone we meet—some ready sympathy, a quick eye, and a little tact are all that are needed.

One of the greatest mistakes of life is to save our smiles and pleasant words and sympathy for those of "our set," or for those not now with us, or for other times than the present.

"If a word or two will render another person happy," said a Frenchman, "he or she must be a wretch indeed who will not give it. It is like lighting another man's candle with your own, which loses none of its brilliancy by what the other gains."

Sydney Smith recommends us to make at least one person happy every day: "Take ten years, and you will make thirty-six hundred and fifty persons happy; or brighten a small town by your contribution to the fund of general joy."

Dr. Raffles once said: "I have made it rule never to be with a person ten minutes without trying to make him happier." It was a remark of Dr. Dwight, that "one who makes a little child happier for half an hour is a fellow-worker with God."

A little boy said to his mother: "I couldn't make little sister happy, nohow I could fix it. But I made myself happy trying to make her happy."

"I make Jim happy, and he laughs," said another boy, speaking of his invalid brother; "and that makes me happy, and I laugh."

There was once a king who loved his little boy very much, and took a great deal of pains to please him. So he gave him a pony to ride, beautiful rooms to live in, pictures, books, toys without number, teachers, companions, and everything that money could buy or ingenuity devise; but for all this, the young prince was unhappy. He wore a frown wherever he went, and was always wishing for something he did not have. At length a magician came to the court. He saw the scowl on the boy's face, and said to the king: "I can make your son happy, and turn his frowns into smiles, but you must pay me a great price for telling him this secret." "All right," said the king; "whatever you ask I will give." The magician took the boy into a private room. He wrote something with a white substance on a piece of paper. He gave the boy a candle, and told him to light it and hold it under the paper, and then see what he could read. Then the magician went away. The boy did as he had been told, and the white letters turned into a beautiful blue. They formed these words: "Do a kindness to some one every day." The prince followed the advice, and became the happiest boy in the realm.

"Happiness," says one writer, "is a mosaic, composed of many smaller stones."

It is the little acts of kindness, the little courtesies, the disposition to be accommodating, to be helpful, to be sympathetic, to be unselfish, to be careful not to wound the feelings, to not expose the sore spots, to be charitable of the weaknesses of others, to be considerate—these are the little things which, added up at night, are found to be the secret of a happy day. How much greater are all these than one great act of noteworthy goodness once a year!

Our lives are made up of trifles; emergencies rarely occur. "Little things, unimportant events, experiences so small as to scarcely leave a trace behind, make up the sum total of life."

"What a gift it is," said Beecher, who was the great preacher of cheerfulness, "to make all people better and happier without knowing it! We do not suppose that flowers know how sweet they are. These roses and carnations have made me happy for a day. Yet they stand huddled together in my pitcher, without seeming to know my thoughts of them, or the gracious work they are doing. This, too, is the portion of person who is a natural heart-singer, a person whose nature is large and luminous, and who, by his or her spontaneous actions, calms, cheers, and helps others. God bless these people, for they bless everybody!"

What a heart gift it must have been to John B. Gough, therefore, when he recounted this incident in his life:

> I was appointed to lecture in a town in Great Britain six miles from the railway and a man drove me in a fly from the station to the town. I noticed that he sat leaning forward in an awkward manner, with his face close to the glass of the window. Soon he folded a handkerchief and tied it round his neck. I asked him if he was cold. "No, sir." Then he placed the handkerchief round his face. I asked him if he had the toothache. "No, sir," was the reply. Still he sat leaning forward. At last I said, "Will you please tell me why you sit leaning forward that way with a handkerchief round your neck if you are not cold and have no toothache?" He said very quietly, "The window of the carriage is broke, and the wind is cold, and I am trying to keep it from you." I said, in surprise, "You are not putting your face to that broken pane to keep the wind from me, are you?" "Yes, sir, I am." "Why do you do that?" "God bless you, sir! I owe everything I have in the world to you." "But I never saw you before." "No, sir; but I have seen you. I was a ballad-singer once. I used to go round with a half-starved baby in my arms for charity, and a draggled wife at my heels, half the time with her eyes blackened; and I went to hear you in Edinburgh, and *you told me I was a man*; and when I went out of that house I said, 'By the help of God, I'll be a man'; and now I've a happy wife and a comfortable home. God bless you, sir! I would stick my head in any hole under the heavens if it would do you any good."

"Live for something," says Dr. Chalmers. "Do good, and leave behind you a monument of virtue which the storms of time can never destroy. Write your name in kindness, love, and mercy on the hearts of those who come in contact with you, and you will never be forgotten, Good deeds will shine as brightly on earth as the stars of heaven."

"There is," says Robert Waters, "no use in living at all if only for oneself. It is not at all necessary for you to make a fortune, but it is necessary, absolutely necessary, that you should become a fair-dealing, honorable, useful human being, radiating goodness and cheerfulness wherever you go, and making your life a blessing."

And yet, how many of us hoard our gifts? How many of us, sadly, go through our lives with our eyes steadily fixed on a distant goal, straining every nerve to reach it. We pass on our way innumerable opportunities for helping others over rough places, for brightening and beautifying the commonplace life of every day. But we see them not. Heedless of all that does not help us on the line of our own particular ambition, we finally arrive at our destination to find—what? We have gained what we sought, but at the cost of all that sweetens and beautifies, that ennobles and enriches, life.

What makes us think that we are going to do wonderful things tomorrow? Why does today look so void of promise; tomorrow so rosy, so poetic?

What reason have you to believe that you are going to be ideally happy and harmonious, unselfish and helpful at some indefinite time in the future, when today you are uncharitable? How is it that in some distant future you expect to get so much time to write letters to your friends and to those who are sick and discouraged, and to give to your own self-improvement and to broadening your mind, when you can find no time for these things today?

What is there in tomorrow that we think can work such magic of improvement upon today?

Why think that you are some day going to pick up the many things lying about the house—almost useless to you, but which would be valuable to those who are poorer than yourself? That you are going to make up a box of cast-off clothing, books, pictures, and other things, and send them next week or next month to those who really need them? You have not done it in the past, you are not doing so today, why continue promising yourself that you will do so in the future?

How many people, not through stinginess but from sheer thoughtlessness and ignorance of the needs of others, stow things away in cellar or attic that might help to open the way to a great future for some poor boy or girl!

Go up to your attic today. Look in your trunks and about your house and see how many things are lying around that you can not only dispense with, but which are really in your way and would bring a measure of comfort and happiness to others less fortunate than yourself.

Look over your old clothing and pick out the articles that you will never wear again, but which would prove a real godsend to some poor people out of employment, or who have so many depending upon them that they cannot afford to buy necessary clothing for themselves. Do not keep those things until they become useless, thinking you may need them some time. Let them do good *now*, pass them along today. They have served your turn. Let them be messengers of good cheer, evidences of your love and thoughtfulness of others.

There are probably books in your library or lying around the house which no one has looked in for years, or will read for years to come, which would be of inestimable value to boys and girls or men and women who are trying to educate themselves under great difficulties. Pass them on today. The more you give away the more you will have and enjoy. The habit of stinginess strangles happiness; the habit of giving multiplies it.

Do not be selfish, at least with the things that you can spare. Do not hoard them, thinking that you may want them later. You can make an infinitely greater investment in your own character, in satisfaction and happiness, by giving them away than by keeping them in anticipation of some future contingency that will never arise.

Giving will soften your heart and open a little wider the door of your generosity.

A highly cultured and refined woman not long ago told me of her struggles to get a musical education. She was so poor that for a long time she could not afford to purchase or rent any kind of an instrument, and used to practice for hours daily on a piano keyboard which she had marked on a sheet of brown paper. While struggling to get along in this way, she was invited to a dinner at the home of a wealthy family. After dinner she was shown over the house by her hostess, who took her from kitchen to attic.

"And there," she said, "in the attic, I saw, stored away, an old piano, which I would have given anything I had in the world to have possessed. I would have been glad to have walked a long distance every day for the privilege of practicing on it. I cared nothing for the sumptuous dinner, the handsome furniture, the beautiful pictures, and evidences of luxury on every hand, but that old piano, lying unused in the attic, haunted me. It would have opened the door to paradise for me, yet I dared not ask for it."

Give me someone like the elderly lady who was traveling West on a crowded train, and who every little while would take a bottle from her satchel, hold it out of the window and shake something out of it which looked like salt. Unable to restrain his curiosity any longer, the man seated next to her finally asked her what she was doing. "Oh," she said, "these are flower seeds. I have made it a rule for many years when traveling to scatter seeds by the railroad tracks, especially in crossing the desert and in unattractive parts of the country. Do you see those beautiful flowers beside the track? Well, they came from seeds which I scattered along this same road many years ago."

A great philanthropist said that he had saved only what he had given away, that the rest of his fortune seemed lost.

What we give away has a wonderful power of doubling and quadrupling itself on the return bound. It is the greatest investment in the world. It comes back in geometrical progression.

Give! give!! give!!! It is the only way to keep from drying up.

"When I give I give myself," wrote Whitman.

Selfishness is self-destruction. Those who never help anybody, who tightly shut their purses when there is a request to give, who say that all they can do is to attend to their own affairs, who never give a thought to their neighbors, who hug all their resources to themselves, who want to get all and give nothing in return, are those who shrivel and dry up like the rosebud, and who becomes small and mean and contemptible.

We all know those poor dwarfed souls who never give, who close the petals of their helpfulness, withhold the fragrance of their love and sympathy, and in the end lose all they tried to hoard for themselves. They are cold, lifeless, apathetic; all their sympathies have dried up; they cannot enter into the higher and nobler emotions of human life. Their souls have been frozen by selfishness and greed. They have become so narrow and stingy that they fear to give even a kind word or smile lest they may rob themselves of something. They have rendered themselves incapable of radiating sunshine or happiness, and, by the working of an immutable law, they receive none.

A strong man, watching one who was delicate and undeveloped exercising in a gymnasium, said to him: "My dear young man, how foolish you are to waste your energy on those parallel bars and dumbbells. You are weak, physically, and ought to save what strength you have for your day's work. You cannot afford to squander your vitality that way."

"Oh, but, my good sir," replied the other, "you don't see the philosophy underlying this exercise. The only way I can increase my power is by first giving out what I have. I give my strength to this apparatus, but it returns what I give it with compound interest. My muscles grow by giving it out in effort, in exercise."

Give and increase; hoard and lose. It is a universal law of growth.

"I will roll up my petals of beauty," said the selfish rosebud. "I will withhold this precious fragrance, this love incense of sun and dew for myself. "It is wasteful extravagance to give it away to careless passersby." But, behold, the moment it stores up what it has, withholds its riches from others, they vanish, and it shrivels and dies!

"I will give myself out," said the generous rose. "I will bestow my beauty and fragrance on everybody who passes my way." And, lo, it blossoms into a riot of sweetness and loveliness of which it never dreamed. It had only a tiny bit of fragrance until it tried to give that little to the world. Then, to its astonishment, it was flooded with sweet odors that came from somewhere—evolved from the chemistry of the sunlight, the moisture in the air and the chemical forces in the soil.

The habit of doing good, of helping somebody every day, of dropping a little word of encouragement here and there—to a newsboy, a waiter in a restaurant or a hotel, a driver on a bus, a toiler in your home or your office, a poor unfortunate man or woman in a wretched home, or on a seat in the park—this is what broadens and ennobles life, makes character beautiful and fragrant as the rose. This is the sort of giving that returns to us with compound interest.

Everywhere we go we find opportunities for this sort of giving. Everywhere we find some one who needs encouragement, someone whose heart is breaking under a heavy load, someone who needs sympathy, someone who needs a lift. We never can tell what glorious fruitage the seed of the most trivial act of kindness may produce. Many a heart has been cheered simply by a smile from a stranger. A look of sympathy, an expression of a desire to help, a warm grasp of the hand has brought back hope and courage to many a disheartened soul. A kind letter, a word of encouragement has been turning-point in the career of many a person on the verge of despair.

There are gifts more precious than anything money can buy and which are in the power of all to bestow.

The little girl who spent all her pennies in buying paper and a postage stamp to write to her grandmother at Christmas, saying, "I love you, I love you, dear grandmamma," teaches us a splendid lesson. Such salutation will mean more to another than many of the so-called great things. A kind word is the small change of life. Give it out freely. The more you give, the richer you will grow.

Give! give! give *now*, TODAY! Help yourself to grow larger, broader, happier, more useful to humanity as the years go by. *Those only are happy who have their minds fixed on some object other than their own happiness.*

Give, give, give—of whatever you have; but give yourself with your gift. It is love for which the world is hungering. "Scatter your flowers as you go, for you will not pass this way again."

Today I will...

→ *Look around my home. What have you been storing up for a rainy day, and the rains have come and the rains have gone, and you still have those things stored up. Box those things up and give them to some charity, some organization that helps others, some child, some person you know who is doing without.*

→ *Think twice about calling "junk mail" every piece of literature that comes to my home and is a request for a donation to help in some service or cause—to feed the poor, to protect the earth, etc. Pick one that represents a cause you believe in strongly. If you are concerned as to whether or not your contribution will truly go toward the good you intend, research the organization. Find out all you can about it and how it spends its money. If what you find doesn't satisfy you, pick another letter out of the stack that comes monthly and research that organization. Continue doing so until you have found a place to give.*

→ *Remember that money and things aren't all I have to give. There is yourself to give. Volunteer for some worthy organization. Help at a nursing home, at the pound; offer your services to the Special Olympics; find out if there's an organization in your community that reads magazine articles, newspapers, books to the blind and offer to read. Become a Big Brother or Big Sister.*

→ *I will remember that sometimes it's easy to think only of giving to others and forget that "charity begins at home." Call your spouse at work as a surprise and offer to take him or her to lunch. Take your children out to dinner, one at a time; take them someplace where they can "dress up," if that's something they'd enjoy. Offer to help coach a sport that your child plays; or sell tickets, or help in the concession booth at the game. Schedule your time so you're free to attend each event that your children participate in—school plays, orchestral performances, sporting events, etc.*

chapter 8

THE JOYS OF FRIENDSHIP

Friendship is Love without his wings.
—*French proverb*

One reason why so many people are disappointed with what life has for them is that they have never cultivated the capacity for friendship. They seem think that friends are mere incidental things in life, that it is not worth while to put oneself out a great deal to cultivate friendships. And thus it is no surprise that the lives of such people are barren, poverty-stricken, and unsatisfactory.

The intimacy of friendship reveals the deep secrets of our hearts.

Is there anything more sacred in this world than unselfish, devoted friendship, and yet is there anything we take so little pains to cultivate and to keep; is there anything of value we abuse so much by neglect?

One reason why so many people have so few friends is that they have so little to give, and they expect everything. If you cultivate attractive and lovable qualities, friends will flock around you.

Most of us attend to everything else first, and if we have any little scraps of time left we give them to our friends, when we ought to make a business of our friendships. Are they not worth it?

Is there anything more beautiful in this world than the consciousness of possessing sweet, loyal, helpful friends, whose devotion is not affected in the least by a fortune or the lack of it; friends who love us even more in adversity than in prosperity?

The faith of friends is a perpetual stimulus. How it nerves and encourages us to do our best when we feel that scores of friends really believe in us when others misunderstand and denounce us!

Ah, there is no other stimulator, helpmeet, or joy-giver like a true friend! Well might Cicero say: "They seem to take away the sun from the world who withdraw friendship from life; for we have received nothing better from the immortal gods, nothing more delightful."

It means a great deal to have enthusiastic friends always looking out for our interests; working for us all the time; saying a good word for us at every opportunity; supporting us, speaking up for us in our absence when we need a friend; shielding our sensitive, weak spots; stopping slanders; killing lies which would injure us; correcting false impressions; trying to set us right; overcoming the prejudices created by some mistake or slip, or a first bad impression we made in some silly moment; who are always doing something to give us a lift or help us along!

What sorry figures many of us would cut but for our friends!

What a boon our friends are to our weaknesses, our idiosyncrasies and shortcomings, our failures generally! How they throw a mantle of charity over our faults, and cover up our defects!

What a cold, heartless world this would be without our friends—those who believe in us even when everybody else denounces us; those who love us, not for what we *have*, but for what *we are*; those who appreciate us, who help to build up instead of destroying our self-confidence, who double our power of accomplishment; who never embarrass us by making us feel our inferiority or weakness, but, o the contrary, always give us a lift upward, a push onward.

Who can estimate the value of such uplifting influences?

How many people has a strong, loyal friendship has kept from utter despair, from giving up the struggle for success! How many men and women have been kept from suicide by the thought that some one loved them, believed in them; how many have preferred to suffer tortures to dishonoring or disappointing their friends! The thrill of encouragement which has come from the pressure of a friendly hand, or an encouraging, friendly word, has proved the turning-point in many a life.

What is more sacred in this world than those who are friends to us when we are not a friend to ourselves—when we have lost our self-respect, our self-control, our character. Is that not friendship, indeed, which will stand by us when we will not stand by ourselves! I know a man who thus stood by a friend who had become such a slave to drink and all sorts of vice that even his family had turned him out of doors. When his father and mother and wife and children had forsaken him, his friend remained loyal. He would follow him nights in his debauches, and many a time saved him from freezing to death when he was so inebriated that he could not stand. Scores of times this friend would leave his home and hunt in the slums for him, to keep him from the hands of a policeman, to shield him from the cold when every one else had forsaken him. This great love and devotion finally redeemed the fallen man and sent him back to decency and his home. Can any money measure the value of such friendship!

"The purpose of friendship," said Seneca, "is to have one dearer to me than myself, and for the saving of whose life I would gladly lay down my own, taking with me the consciousness that only the wise can be friends; others are mere companions."

And has there ever been such capital for starting in business for oneself as plenty of friends? How many people, who are now successful, would have given up the struggle in some great crisis of their lives, but for the encouragement of some friend which has tided them over the critical place! Many of us would have been very much poorer financially, but for the hosts of friends who have sent us customers and clients and business, who have always turned our way everything they could.

Conversely, one of the saddest phases of our strenuous lives is the terrible slaughter of friendships by chasing after money. Is there anything more chilling in this world than to have a lot of money but practically no friends? What does that thing which we call success amount to if we have sacrificed our friendships, if we have sacrificed the most sacred things in life in getting it? Along the way to our fortunes we may have acquired plenty of acquaintances, but acquaintances are not friends—and we see this most clearly when we realize that there is something that is called friendship which follows us as long as we are prosperous and have anything to give of money or influence, but which forsakes us when we are down.

Real friendship will follow us into the shadows, in the dark as well as in the sunshine. Real friendship is a great test of character. People who lack loyalty have no capacity for great friendship.

Shakespeare tells us how we may distinguish the true from the false friend:

> He that is thy friend indeed,
> He will keep thee in thy need.
> If thou sorrow, he will weep;
> If thou wake, he cannot sleep.
> Thus of every grief in heart,
> He with thee doth bear a part.
> These are certain signs to know
> Faithful friend from flattering foe.

Friendship is no one-sided affair, but an exchange of soul qualities. There can be no friendship without reciprocity. One cannot receive all and give nothing, or give all and receive nothing, and expect to experience the joy and fullness of true companionship.

We only get what we give. Our friends are the harvest of our friendship sowing. If the seed is poor, the harvest is poor. The person who is rich in friendships has sown richly of sympathy, of interest, of admiration, of helpfulness, of love. This is the sowing that gives the bountiful harvest. Those who get all they can from others and give nothing, know not friendship nor real riches.

True friendships are not easy on us; they do not rest upon pretense or deception. Sincerity is the very core of friendship. The friendship which shrinks from telling the truth and cannot bear to cause pain when justice demands it, does not command as high a quality of admiration as the one which is absolutely just, frank, and sincere.

For the honesty when we are deceiving ourselves and leading ourselves astray, for the sustenance when we find the world unmanageable, for the support in times when we are unable to be of support to ourselves, cementing precious friendships, cultivating those we love cannot be surpassed in bringing to us the true and everlasting sources of happiness. Millions of us, indeed, date the beginning of our nobility from the time be acquired certain friendships.

"In friendship lies ever a road to happiness," said Ella Wheeler Wilcox. "It has always been my theory."

"But you will find friends insincere, and friendship but a name," predicted the pessimist.

"You will suffer disillusionment, and it will be more bitter than any friendship can be sweet. Keep to yourself, and avoid the awakening from a useless dream."

"Still I pursued my course. I formed many ties of friendship. Some were broken, and I suffered; but one great truth came home to my heart, to rest there always: In being a true friend, and worthy of true friendship, lies the road to real, lasting happiness."

Today I will…

- → *Call or write those friends who are not near me. Many are heart hungry and miserable for no other reason than this: they are living apart from their friends. There is a balm in friendship that can heal a thousand ills. There is a power in the tender sympathy of a friend that can disperse the darkness of despair and cause the sunshine of hope and cheer to flood the mansion of life once more.*

- → *Do not be afraid to tell your friends that you love them. Tell them of their qualities that you admire. Do not presume too much upon your friendships. Do not allow them to be strained too much either by long absences without communication or without seeing them when it is possible to do so.*

- → *Make a note to express gratitude to my friends on my birthday for their friendship. On our birthdays, we receive gifts and/or cards from our family and friends. On your next birthday, send your friends a card, expressing your gratitude for having them in your life—for their presence in your life having made the very fact that you were born, special.*

- → *Take a friend out to lunch or dinner, for no other reason than that he or she is your friend, and you want to celebrate that.*

chapter 9

JOY IN our WORK

It is in the satisfaction in our work that keeps us in health, contentment, and prosperity.

Most people are looking and hoping for release from work, and yet all history and all experience prove that busy people, people who are constantly occupied, are the happiest. It makes all the difference in the world, however—to our health and happiness—whether we look upon our work as drudgery or whether we do it with delight. Work should be a tonic, not a grind; life a delight, not a struggle.

The late Charles A. Dana fairly bubbled over with the enjoyment of his work, and was, up to his last illness, at his office every day. A Cabinet officer once said to him: "Well, Mr. Dana, I don't see how you stand this infernal grind."

"Grind?" said Mr. Dana. "You never were more mistaken. I have nothing but fun."

"It is worthy of special remark," said Wilhelm von Humboldt, "that when we are not too anxious about happiness and unhappiness, but devote ourselves to the strict and unsparing performance of duty, then happiness comes of itself."

"Those only are happy," it is said truthfully, "who have their minds fixed on some object other than their own happiness."

We ought to carry each day nobly, doing the duty of enjoying the privilege of the moment, without thinking whether or not it will make us happy. This is quite in accord with the saying of George Herbert, "The consciousness of duty performed gives us music at midnight."

And, indeed, what a joy there is an exquisitely done job, a piece of work that is done to the complete finish, that has our unqualified approval. It makes us respect ourselves more! What can give better satisfaction than a sense of mastery in our undertakings?

"It is not work that kills people," said Beecher, "it is worry. Work is healthy; you can hardly put more on a person than he or she can bear. But worry is rust upon the blade. It is not movement that destroys the machine, but friction."

"The unhappiness of life," says Dr. Thomas R. Slicer, "lies in the fret of it—not in work, but in its worry. Good, strong well-ordered work never killed a man; but the worry of it, the loading up of an hour with two hours' work, the loading up of an evening with too many engagements, being avaricious of pleasure and greedy of delight, will make us unhappy. Joy ceases to be joy when it is not conveniently handled and easily carried."

Work ought to be our greatest blessing, for it is the law of nature that anything that is not helpfully occupied begins to deteriorate, to go to pieces. It matters not whether it is an engine or a human brain: exercise or deteriorate is the law of life. The most unhappy person in the world is the one *without* employment; no amount of wealth can take the place of being engagingly employed.

"We must work. That is certain as the sun. But we may work grudgingly or we may work gratefully. We cannot always choose our work, but we can do it in a generous temper, and with an up-looking heart. There is no work so rude that we may not breathe a soul into it; there is no work so dull that we may not enliven it."

No matter what your business may be, if you are an employer, you will find that no investment you can make will pay you so well as the effort to scatter heart sunshine through your establishment. Scolding, fault-finding, criticizing, and slave-driving methods have been tried in every business from the beginning of time and have proved total failures. They have crushed hope out of the most buoyant, strangled enthusiasm, killed spontaneity, and made service for every one in his establishment a dreary drudgery instead of a delight. The employer who easily finds fault and is never generous spirited, who never commends the work of employees when to do so would be just, who is unwilling to brighten their hours, fails to secure the best of himself or herself, as well as of his or her employees.

If you are an employer, do not go about your place of business as though you thought life were a wretched, miserable grind. Show yourself master of the situation, not its slave. Rise above the petty annoyances which destroy peace and harmony. Make up your mind that you are too large to be overcome by trifles. Resolve that you will be larger than your business, that you will overtop it with your character and cheerfulness.

Moreover, is it not your *duty* to make as pleasant and as full of sunshine as possible the lives of those who are helping you to carry on your business? Is that not the best possible policy for you to pursue? We all know that a horse that is prodded all the time by means of whip and spur and rein will not travel nearly so far without becoming exhausted as one that is urged forward by gentleness and kind treatment. In their responsiveness to kindness, men and women are in nowise different from the lower animals. You cannot expect your employees to remain buoyant, cheerful, alert, and unwearied under the goad of scowls and the lash of a bitter tongue. Energy is only another name for enthusiasm, and how can you expect those who work for you to be enthusiastic or energetic in your service when surrounded by an atmosphere of despondency and gloom, when they expect a volley of curses and criticism every time you pass?

Similarly, if as an employee you dislike your position, complain to no one about it, least of all to your employer! Fill the place with your spirit as it was never filled before. Crowd it to overflowing. You will make yourself more content for it. Show that you are abundantly worthy of better things. Express yourself in this manner as freely and often as you can, for it is the only way that will count.

"I have found my greatest happiness in labor," said Gladstone. "I early formed a habit of industry, and it has been its own reward."

It is difficult for many of us to see how we can possibly get happiness out of our monotonous, humdrum vocations, to which we are chained by some necessity or another. We see no consistency or relationship between what is often referred to as the dry, dreary drudgery of work and the idea that life was intended to be a joy, a perpetual delight. We cannot see any correlation between hard work or disagreeable duties and delight. We are unable, unlike the bee, to extract honey from the bitter flowers of life with which we must all have experiences. For many of us, labor and everything alike it that seems a drudgery, is a curse.

We would get a good lesson by studying the bees, who, every minute during the day of the honey season, find sweets in every weed, in poisonous flowers—in things in which we would never think of looking for anything good.

Remember, no one ever found the world quite as he or she would have liked it. You will be sure to have burdens laid upon you that belong to other people. But don't grumble. If the work needs doing and you can do it, never mind about the other one who ought to have done it and didn't. Do it yourself. Those who fill up the gaps and smooth away the rough spots, finish the jobs that others leave undone, are worth a regiment of grumblers.

Every nerve and every muscle, every fiber, every cell in our body, cries out for exercise, for work. The eye wants work, the ear wants work, the perceptions want work; every faculty of the mind calls for healthful exercise.

The perfect heaven which the old theologians and many people once pictured for themselves, would, in reality, make a hell for active, thinking people. What would we do in a place where the streets were paved with gold, the walls made of glass, and where there was perpetual rest? Every cell in our brain calls for activity, and existence in a place where the faculties were lulled to rest would be torture to normal human beings. We are so constituted that we are happiest when we are the most active in useful work.

There is every indication, then, that in the nature of things it was intended that we *should* find our greatest happiness, our great satisfaction in life—our chief joy—in our daily occupation. We should find our soul and delight in it. It should be the conscious self-expression of ourselves. Then the exercise of our powers and faculties would give us constant satisfaction.

We should go to our work in the morning with that keen delight and anticipation that a prospective bride and bridegroom feel on the approach of their wedding day.

What glorious anticipation ambitious artist feel! They can scarcely wait until they can return to the half finished picture which has haunted them since they left it the night before. What if we all approached our work every morning with that supreme zest; with that glorious anticipation of a Michelangelo or a Millet!

With what keen delight authors go to their half-finished book, to take up again the characters which have robbed them of sleep and which have filled their vision through waking hours since they left it the night before.

Every one ought to go to work with a similar zest, with the anticipated joy that can scarcely wait until the store, the factory, or the studio opens in the morning.

Most of us, however, merely exist. We do not really live, because there is not in our vocation any true joy. Our vocation should be our joy. That is the key. But the exercise that comes from our work can only give enjoyment according to the kind and quality of faculties within us that are called into action. If the benevolent faculties, the unselfish faculties are called into play, we get a much higher form of enjoyment than when only the greedy, selfish faculties, or earning-a-living are exercised.

We should be pouring our souls and finding our delight in that which allows us to not only give our best but *be* our best. Merely to grind out a day's work because we have to do it, to work under pressure, is not living.

Miss Alma-Tadema, in her lecture on "What is Happiness?" said it took her five months to write down the definition of happiness. She says that happiness is the result of working hard and developing one's powers to the limit. She does not believe that it is possible for us to be very happy while we are conscious that what we are doing is developing only a small percentage of our possible ability. If the work we are engaged in does not allow us to do our best to give our best, then we will hear the perpetual reprimand of our soul within which will take the edge off our happiness.

Instead of growing up with the idea that earning a living is a disagreeable necessity, we should be taught to feel that the bread and butter side of one's occupation is only a mere incident in one's vocation. The principal reason for an occupation ought to be to pursue the calling in which we manufacture joy as well as a living. We should be taught that we will should look for, and will then find, our Eden of satisfaction in our vocation. We should be trained to think that if we make it a point to find our right place in life, our occupations will be a grand privilege which will bring supreme joy. We should be taught that there is no such thing as drudgery in the work one loves, that it is a perpetual delight, a glorious privilege. Then we would go to our occupations every morning with as keen anticipation as we go to the amusements we love best.

Life means little without a purpose. If our aim is lost, we simply exists—we do not really live. To merely grind out a day's work because we have to do it, to work under pressure of obligation, is not living.

The way to find happiness in work, and thus in our lives, is to determine early in life that our work will not simply be how we busy ourselves or make money, but will truly be our vocation—literally, our calling—for there has yet been a human being who is wretched while wholeheartedly and actively engaged in his or her talent.

Today I will...

- *Find reasons to express gratitude in my work rather than complaint. No matter what the job, no matter what its demands, no matter what you may have to suffer from the people and public you work with, you can still express a spirit of gratitude—you can remind yourself that it was the position you applied for—and your anticipated expression of yourself in it—and not the circumstances. Moreover, in expressing gratitude, you will preserve your sense of dignity, your health—no amount of annoyance in your workplace is worth shortening our life over—and your self-approval.*

- *Remember not to push myself at work beyond my capacity for satisfaction. The trouble is, many of us are tempted to overwork. We strain to do more than we are able. We wear ourselves out where we should be receiving—in satisfaction, in contentment, in fulfillment—even greater than we are giving.*

- *Remember that the true joy in work is not from the money gained, but from the satisfaction gained. Enjoy your accomplishments, today. No matter what more you'll have to do tomorrow, today you did enough, and you did it your best. Give yourself credit, today, for a job well done.*

→ *Remember that if my work is with the public, I am not just serving them, I am helping them—and nobody can do that better than I can. Even if you don't know all the answers to all the questions you might be asked by the people who come to you for business, you can tell them you will be happy to find out what the answers are. Helping and happiness don't have to mean knowing everything, just the willingness to do what you can to find out what you and the customer needs.*

→ *Express joy in my work if for no other reason than that I have work—a place to be; an income that allows me to do many of the things I wish.*

→ _____
_____

→ _____
_____

→ _____
_____

→ _____
_____

chapter 10

AESTHETIC APPRECIATION

I have lov'd the principle of beauty in all things.
-Keats

I believe that the cultivation of the power of esthetic appreciation would alone increase human happiness a thousand percent. Who can estimate what it means to a human being who is a lover of the beautiful to have the door of his or her aesthetic faculties opened! How the early cultivation of the love of the beautiful magnifies all the beautiful things in the world!

But, we can only enjoy what we can appreciate, and our appreciations are along the line of our training, our experiences, and our hereditary tendencies. Sadly, therefore, many go through life beauty-blind, because their aesthetic eyes have never been unsealed. Their minds have been left untrained. There are multitudes of closed doors within many, which, if opened by education, training, and culture, would enrich the lives of these people wonderfully and would lead to untold happiness.

What a treasury of joys—which infinitely surpass all the pleasures which come from material things—is revealed by the opening of the door of aesthetic appreciation! Everything in life is loaded with some special meaning, but will only give up its secret to the soul that responds to it, the soul that has an affinity for it. How much around us is ready to speak in beauty to those who have a spiritual responsiveness which can interpret its divine meaning! Then, no matter how poverty-stricken our environment may be, no matter what misfortunes, failures, distressing circumstances might surround or befall us, it is always possible to rise out of these discords into a heaven of unspeakable joy.

Even the barred cell cannot confine such a mind from the joys of happiness and beauty, as exemplified by the famous lines which the English poet Lovelace wrote to Althea while he was in prison to Althea:

Stone walls do not a prison make,
Nor iron bars a cage;
Minds innocent and quiet take
That for an hermitage;
If I have freedom in my love,
And in my soul am free,
Angels alone that soar above
Enjoy such liberty.

Benjamin West said that it was his mother's kiss in appreciation of a little drawing of his that made him a painter. It was this kiss, he said, that opened up a new world to him—the world beautiful.

Many an artist's soul has been set on fire by looking upon another's masterpiece which started the conflagration in the artist's aesthetic nature, and which thereafter was never quenched. ("I too am a painter," cried Correggio when he beheld Raphael's St. Cecilia.) Art is unquestionably one of the purest and highest elements in human happiness. "It trains the mind through the eye, and the eye through the mind. As the sun colors flowers, so does art color life."

The study of a flower, of a plant, of a sunset, of a bit of landscape, kindled the flame which fired the aesthetic soul of Ruskin—opened up a new world in the great within of himself, which not only made his own life a joy, but enabled him to open the door of happiness in a vast multitude of other lives. And just once open this door of appreciation in a human soul and no power in heaven or earth can ever close it again, nor limit the possibilities in the discovery.

Beauty is a refining, elevating, saving force. The love of the beautiful is an indication that the possessor has risen into the upper stories of life, where he or she has caught a glimpse of his or her God.

Our souls were not intended to be imprisoned; nor be weighed down by unfortunate conditions. Our intellectual and beauty-creating powers were given, in part, as a means of escape from the most discouraging, distressing surroundings. No failure, no disaster from fire or flood, can keep any of us from rising into a paradise of harmony and beauty where our souls can revel in a world of their own making—equipped, decorated by our own creative imagination.

What you can abstract from life is just a question of how you train your mind and form your habits of thought. It is just a question of your ability to extract beauty, utility, and joy from your environment, which you think is so commonplace, dry, lean, and void of beauty. As Martin Luther said, paradise might apply to the whole world—and why not? There is not a corner of the Universe which the great Lover of the Beautiful has not decorated with more marvelous beauties than any human being ever decorated anything. In the far-away places where no human being has ever trod, there are beauties of plant life, of flowers, of crystal formation in rocks, beauties of birds and beast, of landscape, which no human eye bath ever seen, proving that the great Author of the Universe is a lover of "uncontained immortal beauty." What a pity that every child should not be taught to read "God's handwriting in beauty" in everything—everywhere!

"More servants wait on man/Than he'll take notice of," wrote the English metaphysical poet and Anglican priest, George Herbert.

If you think your life has so little for you, you have not learned the secret of extracting from life its joys, beauties, truth, and love-liness. The soul that loves beauty can feast on it everywhere. There is not a nook or corner in the universe where it does not exist. "I wandered lonely as a cloud," wrote Wordsworth, "That floats on high o'er vales and hills, when all at once I saw a crowd—a host, of golden daffodils."

What golden opportunities surround us for coining our bits of leisure into aesthetic indulgences that will mean growth of character, promotion, advancement, power, and riches that no accident can take from you, no disaster annihilate!

Even in the poorest of neighborhoods there are still the stars and moon overhead, the laughter of a child, the beauty in another's eyes. And how often do we see even in the most otherwise drab circumstances, the evidence of beauty in a single flower—or even a colorful weed—straining to rise from the cracks of a sidewalk.

No matter which way we look we can see marvels of design, of possible utility and of beauty, which a whole lifetime of study could never exhaust.

"To watch the corn grow, or the blossoms set; to draw hard breath over ploughshare or spade; to read, to think, to love, to pray; these," said Ruskin, "are the things that make men and women happy."

Suppose the greatest human being that ever lived could be endowed with the omnipotence, the omniscience, the magic power and the wisdom, to create a world which in every particular would be a paradise, a world which would be absolutely perfect in every respect; to evolve a plant life which would give the greatest possible joy and satisfaction to human beings; create fruits, vegetables and all else which would give the most intense pleasure to the human palate. In other words, suppose this human being should be endowed with God-like qualities to create a world which could satisfy every yearning and every longing of the soul. Does this human being not already exist within each of us in our imaginative faculties at this very moment! Can you not now shut your eyes to all that is worrisome about you and envision a word sublime?

A great admirer of the Swiss-American zoologist and geologist Agassiz once sent him a check for one thousand dollars so that he could travel abroad and collect some valuable material and bring home precious truths for his wonderful science. But Agassiz wrote him that he proposed to spend his vacation in his own backyard—and his great mind found even there remnants of fossil remains and other discoveries which made valuable additions to science. The mind which could profitably spend days upon the scale of a fish, and hours studying and reading the history of a grain of sand from the seashore and the history of an ocean pebble, could find material enough in the humblest environment for the profitable study of a lifetime.

There is not a single human desire, not a longing which has not been provided for in this marvelous creation. Why, then, is it that our lives are so often so very lean, so poverty-stricken, so pinched, so limited, so blighted, when they might be so grand, so magnificent, so sublime?

The love of the beautiful is a fundamental quality of the human mind. It first manifests itself in the ornate decorations of primitive tribal people, and becomes an increasing passion with the progress of civilization. Merely to exist was not the object of our creation, but to live sublimely, magnificently, to live like a king, not like a manikin, not like a starved, stunted, burlesque of the real person that is possible.

Suppose there are two people—one who sees wonder in every leaf, a divine message in every flower, whose very soul leaps for joy at the sight of every bit of beautiful scenery, whose soul is all aglow in a sunset; the other one who sees in the same only a leaf, only a flower, only the sun dropping below the horizon. The latter will never find happiness if his or her fortunes wane, for his or her opportunity to turn to the joys of aesthetic appreciation pleasure in such times has been stunted and starved.

Surrounded as we are with the real sources of happiness—costless and limitless—many of us nevertheless allow our finer senses to atrophy and turn to money and the material things it can buy us as the primary source of happiness. But putting money into the purse is pretty poor sort of business compared with putting beauty into the life, cultivating the sublime, the magnificent in our natures.

The joy of living lies not *with* us, but *within* us. It is the power to appreciate, to make our own the aesthetic joys that are free and everywhere to all. Happiness or misery is in our own power.

Too often, though, we confound pleasure and happiness. Pleasure is a more temporary enjoyment. It is the fleeting experience of enjoyment, rather than the enduring satisfaction which comes from, say, the appreciation of a good book. The pleasures which come from the gratification of the appetites and passions are as dross compared with the joys which are revealed in the wonderful realm of aesthetic. The joys of the spirit overtop all others.

For the person who has been trained to extract the honey of life from all sorts of sources, who has been trained to use the senses to notice all around him or her that which has been the great source of all art and beauty, the lack of great sums of money can take little away. Circumstances have scant power to rob him or her. For he or she can become a billionaire in cheerfulness, in usefulness, and in nobility of character, and will never want for happiness. As Keats said:

A think of beauty is a joy forever:
Its loveliness increases; it will never
Pass into nothingness; but still will keep
A bower quiet for us, and a sleep
Full of sweet dreams, and health, and quiet breathing.

Today I will...

- *All through our lives, new doors to new joys are constantly being opened up, often by accident. Today, I will keep my eye open for the doors that open to me that reveal secret beauties around me.*

- *There is no spot on earth so dejecting, poverty-stricken, or distressing that one cannot not only summon from the great writings the grandest characters that have lived in history, but find them always at their best—ever ready upon our call to express their best thoughts, their best moods, their finest philosophy, and enrich our lives and add to our aesthetic appreciation and sensibilities. And in this day of free libraries and inexpensive evening schools, we all, rich or poor, have the opportunity to summon into our presence the greatest poets to sing their choicest songs; the great biographers who will repeat the stories of those who have triumphed over want and woe, who have conquered difficulties and won immortal fame; the painters and sculptors who have made the world more sublime through their labors. Today, not only will I get a library card if I don't have one, I will begin frequenting my local, free, public library, where all the great works of art, poetry, music, and literature are at my beck and call.*

- *I will get film for my camera and keep it always available—to take pictures of sunsets, flowers in bloom, autumn colors, clouds, ice sparkling on a tree, the laughter of my own or a neighbor's child. Photographs capture and preserve memories, and memories are aesthetic experiences: experiences that touch the images of beauty within me.*

- *I will put my name on the mailing list of the local art museum(s), orchestra(s), dance group(s), etc. in order to receive announcements of their upcoming shows, performances, special events. I may not always be able to attend, but the announcements will remind me of what is always available to me aesthetically that I find so easy to forget in my world of duties, obligations, and tasks.*

➔ *I will put a plant in my office, flowers in my kitchen window, have candles on my dinner table, light incense in the rooms of my home—to keep myself in touch with the sweet fragrances and delicate natural beauties in life.*

➔ _____
_____

➔ _____
_____

➔ _____
_____

➔ _____
_____

chapter 11

THE MAN WHO COULDN'T AFFORD A VACATION

Oh, that I had wings like a dove!
For then would I fly away, and be at rest.
—Psalms 55:6

No man or woman can work every day, year in and year out, with no change, no variety in life, without either getting into a rut which will paralyze their finest and best faculties, or by breaking down altogether and shortening their years of precious life.

A great many people, especially in cities, fail, lose their health, and become mere apologies of the men and women they might be if they knew how to take care of themselves—if they were wise enough to take a vacation when they need it. Buried in schemes of ambition, in dreams of wealth and power and fame, they grind away until they become nervous, worn-out wrecks—living on their nerves, trying all sorts of patent medicines, massage treatments, and other artificial remedies, in the hope of regaining health and strength. They do not see the necessity of change; they do not believe in taking a vacation; they laugh at the idea of giving up their work and going away to "idle somewhere," as they put it—until it is too late.

How much money would you give a physician if that doctor would guarantee you strong, steady, healthy faculties, instead of nervous, exhausted ones; if he or she could restore elasticity to your lagging footsteps; give you firm, vigorous muscles instead of weak, flabby ones; put new courage and hope into your life; take away, by some magic, the fretful, nervous feelings which often make you irritable; and restore you to your usual cool, calm, collected, cheerful demeanor?

You would not stop at any price you could afford to pay. Yet you can do all this yourself if you will only drop everything and leave your workplace for rest, change, and complete emancipation from business cares—for the time be to recuperate and to grow strong.

A great many business and professional people are practically slaves to their vocation. They are a part of its machinery. They have become victims of routine. They do what they do today because they did it yesterday. It is easier to go back to the accustomed task than to make a change of any kind, no matter how much they may need it.

I have lived for years near a man who says he never could afford to take a vacation. I have called at his office a great many times, but have never found him at leisure; he is always on the grind; there is no let up in his work from one year's end to another; he believes in the gospel of hard, unremitting work for himself and everybody around him. He says that all this talk about rest and vacation is nonsense; that time taken from business is time wasted; that life is too short for one to go out into the country and sit around doing nothing.

The result is that his close application to work through all these years has broken down his health. His hand trembles so that he can scarcely sign a check. His once vigorous, firm step has given way to an uncertain, lagging one, and there are evidences of weakness in his very bearing. He gives you the impression of a man who is just about to collapse, yet he refuses to give up work or to take a vacation. Although the man has made money, he is a complete failure. None of those who work for him sympathize with him, because they think he is too mean and stingy to take a rest. His family as well as his employees avoid him, because he has become so crabbed and disagreeable. He is a mere business machine—hard, cold, and unresponsive to human emotions. If one were to show him a picture of himself as he really is—as the years of grind and drudgery have made him—he would not believe it was a true one. He thinks he is the same free, open-hearted, generous fellow that he was in his youth.

Everywhere we see duplicates of this man who could not afford to take a vacation.

Eventually, we see this person at hot springs, sulphur springs—all sorts of mineral springs—trying to recover what he or she bartered for a mess of pottage. We see this person taking on steamships and yachts seeking health on the ocean; traveling from place to place, consulting the world's great specialists, trying to get back the vigor and vitality that was lost in exchange for the money that was made while toiling along year after year without rest or change.

The brain will very quickly tell you when it needs a vacation. When it demands a change, it will give you signs that cannot be mistaken. It will humiliate you often enough and make you wonder whether or not you are a real man or woman, when you lose your self-control and fly into a rage over the merest trifles; when you have to force yourself to the work that was formerly a delight; when you begin to feel dull and languid and irritable; when your ambition and enthusiasm begin to wane when your head aches, your eye loses its luster, and your step its elasticity.

These are Nature's reminders that you must stop—or take the consequences. If you do not heed her warnings she will make you pay the penalty—perhaps even with your life. Beware how you presume to do what Nature prohibits. Whether king or beggar, it is all the same to her. She will warn you once, twice, thrice, perhaps oftener, but from her final sentence there is no appeal.

Many a person has been carried to their rest in a hearse years before their natural span of life was run, because they put off their vacation until they could "afford the time"—because they thought they could not afford a few weeks' vacation every year.

Does it pay to take a vacation?

- Does it pay to regain your cheerful personality?

- Does it pay to increase your creative power and originality?

- Does it pay to get a firmer grip on your business or profession?

- Does it pay to regain your lost confidence by up-building your health?

- Do you want to get rid of the scars and stains of the year's campaign?

- Will a fresh, vigorous brain serve you better than a fagged, jaded one?

- Does it pay to exchange flaccid, stiffened muscles for strong, elastic ones?
- Does it pay to get a new grip upon life and to double your power to do good work?
- Does it pay to put iron into the blood and to absorb granite strength from the everlasting hills?
- Does it pay to renew the buoyancy and light-heartedness, the spontaneity and enthusiasm of youth?
- Does it pay to get rid of your nagging, rasping disposition so that you can attract people instead of repelling them?
- Does it pay to get rid of some of our narrow prejudices, hatreds, and jealousies that are encouraged by the strenuous city life?
- Does it pay to add to the comfort and happiness of ourselves and those about us by being brighter and more cheerful ourselves?
- Does it pay to make the most of all the powers that God has given you by bringing superb health and vitality to your aid in developing them?
- Does it pay to develop our powers of observation; to learn to read "books in the running brooks, sermons in stones, and good in everything?"
- Does it pay to put beauty into the life, to gather serenity and poise from the sweet music of the running brooks and the thousand voices in Nature?
- Is it better to be a full-rounded man or woman with large views and a wide outlook, or a mere automatic machine running in the same old grooves year after year?
- Is it a good investment to exchange a few dollars for a great deal of health and happiness; to economize on that on which the very wellsprings of our being depend?
- Does it pay to be free, for a time, from the petty annoyances that vex, hinder, and exasperate; to get out of ruts and the old beaten tracks and take in a stock of brand-new ideas?

- Does it pay to get away from the hot bricks and mortar of the city; to become rejuvenated and refreshed by breathing the untainted and invigorating air of the country?

- Is it better to go to your work with a hopeful outlook or to drag yourself to it like an unwilling slave; to go through life halting, weak, inefficient, pessimistic, or to be strong, vigorous, self-reliant and optimistic?

- Does it pay to save five per cent of your income by economizing on your vacation this year and break down next year from the continued strain and be obliged to pay fifty per cent for doctor's bills, besides the time lost in enforced idleness?

- Does it pay the hard-worked, nerve-racked, desk-bound man to lock his business cares in his office or store and be free once more; to exchange exhausted and irritable nerves for sound, healthy ones, which will carry pleasurable sensations instead of rasping ones?

Growth and power, strength and efficiency must be our aim. To do our best, we must be healthy, strong. If we grind incessantly, this is impossible.

Today I will…

→ *Remind myself that life went on before me, and life will go on after me: I am not indispensable to life, only to myself and my loved ones—and if I do not spend time with myself and them, then I am not even indispensable to them.*

→ *I can take time off from work … everything will be okay, and I will be the better for it. Many of us are afraid to take time off from work because we feel that we are essential. We may be important, but none of us is essential. If we were, the company we work for could not have begun without us, all departments could not continue running without us, and if we were to die tomorrow, everything would stop without us. For very few, if any, of us, is this true. We may also be reluctant to take time off from work because the project we're working on is nearing completion, and we're concerned that we might not receive our just recognition if we're not present. If that's truly a concern, then it's not our vacation we should be questioning, but our workplace circumstances.*

➔ *Remind myself that I do my work, but I am not my work. No matter how much you love your work, not matter how much joy and satisfaction and fulfillment you receive from it, there is more to you than your work. There is the part of you that enjoys a good movie, good conversation, and friends; there is the part of you that wants to be loved and give love; there is the part of you that looks forward to certain special moments with the person you love; there is the part of you that takes pride in your children; there is the part of you that likes certain cities, certain places in nature, etc. This is what vacations are for: to take the time to immerse yourself as completely in expanding, developing, and experiencing those other important and essential facets of your character as you do the rest of the year in work.*

➔ _____
_____

➔ _____
_____

➔ _____
_____

➔ _____
_____

chapter 12

LET IT GO

Better far that my body should suffer outrage than my soul.
—Hroswitha of Gandersheim (first German woman poet)

Do not hang on to the things that keep you back, that make you unhappy. Let go of the worry; let go of the anxiety; let go of the scolding, fretting, and fuming; let go of criticism; let go of fear; let go of the anxious, overstrenuous life; let go of selfish living; let go of the rubbish, the useless, the foolish, the silly; let go of the shams, the shoddy, the false; let go the straining to keep up appearances; let go of the superficial; let go of the vice that cripples, the false thinking that demoralizes; and you will be surprised to see how much lighter and freer and truer you are to run the race, and how much surer of the goal.

If you have had an unfortunate experience, forget it. If you have made a failure in your speech, your song, your book, your article; if you have been placed in an embarrassing position; if you have fallen and hurt yourself by a false step; if you have been slandered an abused, do not dwell upon it. There is not single redeeming feature in these memories, and the presence of their ghosts will rob you of many a happy hour. There is nothing in it. Drop them. Wipe them out of your mind forever. If you have been indiscreet, imprudent; if you have been talked about; if your reputation has been injured so that you fear you can never outgrow it or redeem it, do not drag the hideous shadows, the rattling skeletons about with you. Rub them off from the slate of memory. Wipe them out. Forget them. Start with a clean slate and spend all your energies in keeping it clean for the future.

Resolve that whatever you do or do not do, you will not be haunted by skeletons, that you will not cherish shadows. They must get out and give place to the sunshine. Determine that you will have nothing to do with discords, that every one of them must get out of your mind. No matter how formidable or persistent, wipe them out. Forget them. Have nothing to do with them. Do not let the little enemies—worry and fear, anxiety and regret—sap your energy, for this is your capital for future achievement.

A gloomy face, a sour expression, a worrying mind, a fretting disposition, are proofs of your failure to control yourself. They are the earmarks of your weakness, a confession of your inability to cope with your environment. Drive them away. Scatter them to the four winds. Dominate yourself. Do not let your enemies sit on the throne. Do your own governing.

Dismiss from your mind every suggestion that has to do with illness. If you have had an operation, it is over—let it glide into the shadows, the background of memory. Do not dwell upon it, do not talk about it.

Whatever is disagreeable, whatever irritates, nags, destroys your balance of mind, forget it—thrust it out. It has nothing to do with you now. You have better use for your time than to waste it in regrets, in worry, in useless trifles. Let go the rubbish. Make war upon despondency, if you are subject to it. Drive the "blues" out of your mind as you would a thief out of your house. Shut the door in the face of all your enemies, and keep it shut. Do not wait for cheerfulness to come to you. Go after it: entertain it; never let it go.

The trouble with many of us is that we do not know how to let go of the aches and pains, the anxieties, and just enjoy ourselves. We cannot bear to let go. We cling like a foolish people who cannot bear to throw away a rag or a scrap of anything, but instead piles the useless rubbish in the attic.

We cannot bear to let go of our enemies. We cannot seem to kick out of doors the things that worry and fret and chafe, and yet never do us any good.

We keep our muscles tense and our nerves up to such a pitch that it is the hardest thing in the world for us to drop things. We chafe and worry and fret—haunted by the skeletons of care, of anxiety, and of business—instead of just resting.

Most of us make our backs ache carrying useless, foolish burdens. We carry luggage and rubbish that are of no earthly use, but which sap our strength and keep us jaded and tired to no purpose.

If we could only learn to hold on to the things worthwhile and drop the rubbish—let go of the useless, the foolish, the silly, the things that hinder—we would not only make progress, but we would find our lives infinitely more happy and harmonious as well.

Today I will...

→ *Surrender, take a stress break. When things become overwhelming, seem insurmountable and unsolvable, it's all right to just throw up your hands and say, "Okay, that's it for today!" Don't keep flailing away at a problem that won't budge, or you'll ultimately be flogging yourself.*

→ *Ask for help if I need it. You don't have to know all the answers; you don't have to be perfect. Ask another person for help: it will relieve you of the need to be flawless and it will give the other person an opportunity to feel of value.*

→ *Remind myself that failure is not always the lack of persistence, it is sometimes the lack of letting go.*

→ _____

→ _____

→ _____

→ _____

chapter 13

LAUGHTER

Laugh, and the world laughs with you;
Weep, and you weep alone
—*Ella Wheeler Wilcox*

If people only knew the medicinal power of laughter, of good cheer, of the constant unrepressed expression of joy and gladness, half the physicians would be out of work.

Dr. Ray, superintendent of Butler Hospital for the Insane, wrote in one of his reports, "A hearty laugh is more desirable for mental health than any exercise of the reasoning faculties."

The London *Lancet*, the most eminent medical journal in the world, gives the following scientific testimony to the value of joviality:

> "This power of 'good spirits' is a matter of high moment to the sick and weakly. To the former, it may mean the ability to survive; to the latter, the possibility of outliving, or living in spite of, a disease. It is, therefore, of the greatest importance to cultivate the highest and most buoyant frame of mind which the conditions will admit. The same energy which takes the form of mental activity is vital to the work of the organism. Mental influences affect the system; and a joyous spirit pot only relieves pain, but increases the momentum of life in the body."

Laughter is undoubtedly one of Nature's greatest tonics. It brings the disordered faculties and functions into harmony; it lubricates the mental bearings and prevents the friction which monotonous, exacting business engenders. It is a divine gift bestowed upon us as a life-preserver, a health-promoter, a joy-generator, a success-maker.

I read the other day of a man in a neighboring city who was given up to die. His relatives were sent for, and they watched at his bedside. But an old acquaintance, who called to see him, assured him smilingly that he was all right and would soon be well. He talked in such a strain that the sick man was forced to laugh; and the effort so roused his system that he rallied, and was soon well again.

Was it not Shakespeare who said that a light heart lives long?

The San Francisco *Argonaut* says that a woman in Milpites, a victim of almost crushing sorrow, despondency, indigestion, insomnia, and kindred ills, determined to throw off the gloom which was making life so heavy a burden to her, and established a rule that she would laugh at least three times a day, whether occasion was presented or not; so she trained herself to laugh heartily at the least provocation, and would retire to her room and make merry by herself. She was soon in excellent health and buoyant spirits; her home became a sunny, cheerful abode.

It was said, by one who knew this woman well, and who wrote an account of the case for a popular magazine, that at first her husband and children were amused at her, and while they respected her determination because of the griefs she bore, they did not enter into the spirit of the plan. "But after awhile," said this woman to me, with a smile, only yesterday, "the funny part of the idea struck my husband, and he began to laugh every time we spoke of it. And when he came home, he would ask me if I had had my 'regular laughs'; and he would laugh when he asked the question, and again when I answered it.

"My children, then very young, thought 'mamma's notion very queer,' but they laughed at it just the same. Gradually, my children told other children, and they told their parents.

"My husband spoke of it to our friends, and I rarely met one of them but he or she would laugh and ask me 'How many of your laughs have you had today?' Naturally, they laughed when they asked, and of course that set me laughing.

"When I formed this apparently strange habit I was weighed down with sorrow, and my rule simply lifted me out of it. I had suffered the most acute indigestion; for years I have not known what it is. Headaches were a daily dread; for over six years I have not had a single pain in the head. My home seems different to me, and I feel a thousand times more interest in its work. My husband is a changed man. My children are called 'the girls who are always laughing,' and, altogether, my rule has proved an inspiration which has worked wonders."

"Away with those who go howling through life," wrote Beecher, "and all the while passing for birds of paradise!"

Who are the "lemon-squeezers of society"? They are people who predict evil, extinguish hope, and see only the worst side—"people whose very look curdles the milk and sets your teeth on edge." They are often worthy people who think that pleasure is wrong; people, said an old divine, who lead us heavenward and stick pins into us all the way. They say depressing things and do disheartening things. They chill prayer-meetings, discourage charitable institutions, injure commerce, and kill churches. They are blowing out lights when they ought to be kindling them.

I once lived in a clergyman's family where I scarcely heard a person laugh in months. It seemed to be a part of the inmates' religions to wear long faces and to be sober-minded and solemn. They did not have much use for this world; they seemed to be living for the world to come; and whenever the minister heard me laugh, he would remind me that I had better be thinking of my "latter end," and preparing for the death which might come at any moment. Laughter was considered frivolous and worldly. And as for playing in the house! It would not be tolerated for an instant.

To those who have lost the laughing habit, I would say, "Lock yourself in your room and practice smiling. Smile at your pictures, furniture, mirror—anything, just so the stiff muscles are brought back into play again."

A person without mirth is like a wagon without springs, in which one jolts over every pebble. With mirth, he or she is like a chariot with springs, riding over the roughest roads and scarcely feeling anything but a pleasant rocking motion.

"We should do something more than simply cultivate a cheerful, hopeful spirit," says a health writer, "we should cultivate a spirit of mirthfulness that is not only easily pleased and smiling, but that indulges in hearty, hilarious laughter; and if this faculty is not well marked in our organization we should cultivate it, being well assured that hearty, body-shaking laughter will do us good."

In a corner of his desk, Lincoln kept a copy of the latest humorous work, and it was his habit when fatigued, annoyed, or depressed, to take this up and read a chapter for relief.

"A merry heart," it is said, "maketh a cheerful countenance." Joyfulness keeps the heart and face young. A good laugh makes us better friends with ourselves and everybody around us, and puts us into closer touch with what is best and brightest in our lot in life.

Physiology tells the story. The great sympathetic nerves are closely allied; and when one set carries bad news to the head, the nerves reaching the stomach are affected, indigestion comes on, and one's countenance becomes doleful. Laugh when you can; it is a cheap medicine.

Merriment is a philosophy not well understood. The eminent surgeon Chavasse says that we ought to begin with the babies and train children to habits of mirth:

"Encourage your child to be merry and laugh aloud; a good hearty laugh expands the chest and makes the blood bound merrily, along. Commend me to a good laugh—not to a little snickering laugh, but to one that will sound right through the house. It will not only do your child good, but will be a benefit to all who hear, and be an important means of driving the blues away from a dwelling. Merriment is very, catching, and spreads in a remarkable manner, few being able to resist its contagion. A hearty laugh is delightful harmony; indeed, it is the best of all music."

"Children without hilarity," says an eminent author, "will never amount to much. Trees without blossoms will never bear fruit."

Hufeland commends the ancient custom of jesters at the king's table, whose quips and cranks would keep the company in a roar.

Did not Lycurgus set up the god of laughter in the Spartan eating-halls? There is no table sauce like laughter at meals. It is the great enemy of dyspepsia.

How wise are the words of the acute Chamfort, that the most completely lost of all days is the one in which we have not laughed!

"A crown, for making the king laugh," was one of the items of expense which the historian Hume found in a manuscript of King Edward II.

"It is a good thing to laugh, at any rate," said Dryden, the poet, "and if a straw can tickle a man, it is an instrument of happiness."

"I live," said Laurence Sterne, one of the greatest of English humorists, "in a constant endeavor to fence against the infirmities of ill-health and other evils by mirth; I am persuaded that every time a man smiles—but much more so when he laughs—it adds something to his fragment of life."

"Give me an honest laugher," said Sir. Walter Scott, and he was himself one of the happiest men in the world, with a kind word and pleasant smile for every one, and everybody loved him.

"How much lies in laughter!" exclaimed the critic Carlyle. "It is the cipher-key wherewith we decipher the whole man. Some men wear an everlasting barren simper; in the smile of others lies the cold glitter, as of ice; the fewest are able to laugh what can be called laughing, but only sniff and titter and snicker from the throat outward, or at least produce some whiffing, husky cachinnation, as if they were laughing through wool. Of none such comes good."

"The power to laugh, to cease work and begin to frolic and make merry in forgetful-ness of all the conflict of life," says Campbell Morgan, "is a divine bestowment upon man."

Laughter is a very important element in a successful career. "My young partners do the work and I do the laughing, and I commend to you the thought that there is very little success where there is little laughter," says Andrew Carnegie.

Many who could have been successful sleep in failure's grave today because they took life too seriously.

They poisoned the atmosphere around them so that it became unhealth, and paralyzed their own powers.

WHY DON'T YOU LAUGH?

From the "Independent"

"Why don't you laugh, young man, when troubles come,
Instead of sitting 'round so sour and glum?
You cannot have all play,

    And sunshine every day;
When troubles come, I say, why don't you laugh?

"Why don't you laugh? 'Twill ever help to soothe
The aches and pains. No road in life is smooth;
    There's many an unseen bump,
    And many a hidden stump
O'er which you'll have to jump. Why don't you laugh?

"Why don't you laugh? Don't let your spirits wilt;
Don't sit and cry because the milk you've spilt;
    If you would mend it now,
    Pray let me tell you how
Just milk another cow! Why don't you laugh?

"Why don't you laugh, and make us all laugh, too,
And keep us mortals all from getting blue?
    A laugh will always win;
    If you can't laugh, just grin,
Come on, let's all join in! Why don't you laugh?"

  The world is a looking-glass which flings back to us the reflection of ourselves. If we laugh it laughs back at us. If we shed tears, it reflects a sorrowful face.

  And if refined manners reprove us a little for ill-timed laughter, then at the least a smiling face kindled by a smiling heart is always in order. A smile is said to be to the human countenance what sunshine is to the landscape. Or a smile is called the rainbow of the face. When we lose the power to smile, what hideous images arise in the mind! How soon our imaginations become morbid! When joy goes out, melancholia enters.

  We should not look upon fun and humor as transitory things, but as solid, lasting, permanent, medicinal influences on our whole character.

  A farmer in Alabama, subject to lung trouble, had a hemorrhage while ploughing one day and lost so much blood that he was told by his physician that he would die. He merely said that he was not ready to die yet, and lingered for a long time, unable to get up. He gained strength, and finally could sit up, and then he began to laugh at anything and everything. He persisted in his hilarity, even when well people could see nothing to laugh at, and gained constantly. He became robust and strong. He says he is sure that if he had not laughed continually he would have died.

A great many people have brought sick, discordant bodies back into harmony by "the laugh cure," by substituting cheerfulness for fretting, worrying, and complaining. Every time we complain or finds fault, we are only acknowledging the power of our enemies to hold us down, to make our lives uncomfortable and disagreeable. The way to get rid of these enemies of happiness, is to deny their existence, to drive them out of the mind, for they are only delusions. Harmony, health, beauty, success—these are the realities; their opposites are only the absence of the real.

Why should not having a good time form a part of our daily program? Why should not this enter into our great life plan? Why should we be serious and gloomy because we have to work for a living?

Martin Luther has told us that he was once sorely discouraged and vexed at himself, the world, and the Church, and at the small success he then seemed to be having; and he fell into a despondency which affected all his household. His good wife, could not charm it away by cheerful speech or acts. At length she hit upon this happy device, which proved effectual. She appeared before him in deep mourning.

"Who is dead?" asked Luther. "Oh, do you not know, Martin? God in heaven is dead."

"How can you talk such nonsense, Käthe? How can God die? Why, He is immortal, and will live through all eternity."

"Is that really true?" she persisted, as if she could hardly credit his assertion that God still lived.

"How can; you doubt it? So surely as there is a God in heaven," asserted the aroused theologian, "so sure is it that He can never die."

"And yet," said she demurely, in a tone which made him look up at her; "though you do not doubt there is a God, you became hopeless and discouraged as if there were none It seemed to me you acted as if God were dead."

The spell was broken; Luther heartily laughed at his wife's lesson, and her ingenious way of presenting it. "I observed," he remarked, "what a wise woman my wife was, who mastered my sadness."

Today I will...

→ *Allow myself to laugh—not just chuckle, not just smile, not just laugh to be polite, but laugh with my whole being, especially my heart.*

→ *Not go to bed without having laughed. Make a special point to read from a humorous book, watch a comedy movie or television program, visit a friend who always makes you laugh, if things have not gone well for you this day.*

→ *Bring a laugh into at least one other person's life. No one can have too much laughter, and if you carry laughter to others, you carry laughter within yourself.*

→ *Not take myself so seriously that I cannot laugh at some of my mistakes, faux pas, blunders, etc. We all do silly things, but we too often only let others find the humor in them. If you make some mistake and storm about being vehemently upset with yourself, you can be that somewhere, someone will be laughing at how seriously you're taking yourself. Why not let that person be you?*

→ _____
_____
→ _____
_____
→ _____
_____
→ _____
_____

chapter 14

SINGING

*We must laugh and we must sing,
We are blest by everything,
Everything we look upon is blest.*
—Yeats

I do sing because I must. —Tennyson

Let us cry with Carlyle: "Give us, oh, give us the person who sings at work! Such a person will do more in the same time, will do it better, will persevere longer. One is scarcely sensible of fatigue whilst he or she marches to music. The very stars are said to make harmony as they revolve in their spheres."

"It is a good sign," wrote a writer of earlier times, "when girlish voices carol over the steaming dish-pan or the mending-basket, when the broom moves rhythmically, and the duster flourishes in time to some brisk melody. We are sure that the dishes shine more brightly, and that the sweeping and dusting and mending are more satisfactory because of this running accompaniment of song. Father smiles when he hears his girl singing about her work, and mother's tired face brightens at the sound. Brothers and sisters, without realizing it, perhaps, catch the spirit of the cheerful worker."

At one time, and perhaps still to this day, there were singing milkers in Switzerland. A milkmaid or man received better wages if gifted with a good voice, for a cow yielded one-fifth more milk when soothed by a pleasing melody.

It has also been said that even sheep fatten better to the sound of music. And when field hands are singing, as you sometimes hear in the old country, you maybe sure their labor is lightened.

It was Mrs. Howitt who has told us of the musical bells of the farm teams in a rural district in England: "It was no regular tune, but a delicious melody in that soft, sunshiny air, which was filled at the same time with the song of birds. Angela had heard all kinds of music in London, but this was unlike anything she had heard before, so soft, and sweet, and gladsome. On it came, ringing, ringing as softly as flowing water. The boys and grandfather knew what it meant. Then it came in sight—the farm team going to the mill with sacks of corn to be ground, each horse with a little string of bells to its harness. On they came, the handsome, well-cared-for creatures, nodding their heads as they stepped along; and at every step the cheerful and cheering melody rang out."

"Do all horses down here have bells?" asked Angela.

"By no means," replied her grandfather. "They cost something; but if we can make labor easier to a horse by giving him a little music, which he loves, he is less worn by his work, and that is a saving worth thinking of. A horse is a generous, noble-spirited animal, and not without intellect, either; and he is capable of much enjoyment from music."

A spirit of song, if not the singing itself, is a constant delight to us. "It is like passing sweet meadows alive with bobolinks."

"Some people," said Beecher, "move through life as a band of music moves down the street, flinging out pleasures on every side, through the air, to every one far and near who can listen; others fill the air with harsh clang and clangor. Many people go through life carrying their tongue, their temper, their whole disposition so that wherever they go, others dread them. Some fill the air with their presence and sweetness, as orchards in October days fill the air with the perfume of ripe fruit."

Don't let your music die out while you are struggling daily. For in the end, it is not what you are struggling after but the music within you that will truly enrich your character and add to your soul's worth.

Today I will...

- *Sing more often; I will celebrate myself. "I celebrate myself and sing myself," wrote Whitman, "and what I assume you shall assume." If you are not able to sing at your workplace, then sing at home.*

- *Will not worry if I sing off-key; I will not let others stifle your song because of it. We all have songs in our hearts, and we are better for singing them—whether we sing them in tune or not. "I can't sing," wrote Artemus Ward. "As a singist, I am not a success. I am saddest when I sing. So are those who hear me. They are sadder even than I am." If you can't carry a tune, sing anyway—and laugh with those who wince or laugh at you.*

- *When it's appropriate, when no one else is home who might be disturbed and your neighbors aren't home, turn up your music loudly and sing equally loudly. Let your voice carry to every corner of your home. Let your songs be waiting for you in every room.*

- *Take music lessons. Learn to play the guitar. The basic chords are easy enough to learn (look at how many people have learned to play the guitar!). Then take your guitar with you to the mountains, to parks, to the beach—and sing. Softly, if you prefer, but sing. Don't leave your songs behind you in life.*

chapter 15

LIVING TODAY IN THE HERE AND NOW

*Happy the man and happy he alone
He who can call today his own;
He who's secure within can say,
Tomorrow do thy worst, for I have lived today.*
—Dryden

If an inhabitant of some other planet were to visit America, that visitor would find very few people actually living in the here and the now. He or she would find that most people's gaze is fixed upon something beyond, something to come. They are not really settled today, do not really live in the *now*. Instead, the speak of tomorrow or next year when business is better, their fortunes greater, when they move into their new house, get their new furnishings, their new automobile, get rid of things that now annoy, and have everything around them to make them comfortable. *Then* they will be happy. But they are not really enjoying themselves today.

Our eyes are so focused upon the future, upon some goal in the beyond, that we do not see the beauties and the glories all about us. "There is such a thing," said Uncle Eben, "as too much foresight. People get to figuring what might happen the year after next, and let the fire go out and catch their death of cold right where they are."

We have gotten so accustomed to living in anticipation that our eyes seem not suited to be focused on things near us, only those far away. We are living for tomorrow, tomorrow, losing much of our power of to enjoy the here and the now. And then, "when tomorrow comes it still will be tomorrow!"

We are like children chasing a rainbow. If we could only reach it, what delight! We never believe that we have yet reached the years of our finest living, but we always feel sure that that ideal time of life is coming. And while we wait, we spend our time building air-castles.

That same visitor from another planet would find others dwelling on the past, with its rich but lost opportunities, its splendid chances which they have let slip by.

It is astonishing what new virtues and forces we are able to see and to develop in regretful retrospection, the moment these moments have passed beyond our reach. What splendid opportunities stand out after they have gone by! What could we could do with them if we only had them back!

To be happy, we must learn to let go, to erase, to bury, to forget everything that is disagreeable, that calls up unpleasant memories. These things can do nothing for us but sap the very vitality which we need for correcting our mistakes and misfortunes.

Why should you make yourself miserable by living in the past, by dwelling upon your past mistakes, regretting your failure to seize the opportunities which you think would have made you rich, or blaming yourself for things that have injured you?

I have never known a person to accomplish anything worth-while who was always lashing himself or herself to the past, criticizing and lamenting past blunders, mistakes, and a myriad of other things that had already happened.

It is going to require every bit of energy you can muster to make your life a success—you will not be able to effectively focus your mind on the present with the vigor that accomplishes things when you are thinking or living in the past.

Every bit of force which you expend upon the things which you cannot change is not only thrown away, but leaves you with so much less with which you can eve *compensate* for your unfortunate mistakes and make your future a success. Every particle of force spent in regret is worse than wasted. It does not matter how unfortunate or how black the past has been, it should and can be outlived.

Haul down those black, threatening, deplorable pictures in the mind. They only discourage and incapacitate you from doing good work in the present. Drop from memory the unfortunate error of judgment; forget the unhappy experience, no matter how much it has humiliated or handicapped you. Put your blunders out of mind and resolve to do better in the future.

Nothing is more foolish, nothing more wicked, than to drag the skeletons of the past, the hideous images, the foolish deeds, the unfortunate experiences of yesterday into today's work to mar and spoil it. You may well have been a failure up to the present moment, but you can do wonders in the future if you will only could forget the past, if you will only develop the ability to to cut it off, to close the door on it forever and start anew.

However unfortunate your past has been, forget it. If it throws a shadow upon the present, or causes melancholy or despondency, if there is nothing in it which helps you, then there is not a single reason why you should retain it in your memory and there are a thousand reasons why you should bury it so deeply that it can never be resurrected.

One of the silliest, most inane task any human being is ever guilty of undertaking is that of trying to modify, to change, the unchangeable—whether it be of the past or the future. Our opportunities for happiness are marred by memories of unfortunate mistakes and bitter experiences in an unhappy past—or anticipated improvements in the future.

If we are ever happy, it will be because we create happiness out of our *present* circumstances, with all its vexations, cares, and disheartening conditions. Whoever does not learn to create happiness as he or she goes along—out of the day's work with all its trials, its antagonisms, its obstacles, with all its little annoyances, disappointments—will have missed the great life secret: It is out of the daily round of duties, out of the stress and strain and strife of life—out of this huckstering, buying and selling world—that we must find the honey of life.

The whole world is full of unworked joy mines. Everywhere we go we could find all sorts of happiness-producing material, if we only were determined to extract it. "Everything is worth its while if we only grasp it and its significance. Half the joy of life is, in little things taken on the run."

Do you ever stop to think that the time you are now trying to kill is the very time you once looked forward to so eagerly and which seemed then so precious; that the moments which now hang so heavily on your hands are the same that you then determined should never slip from your grasp until you had extracted from each its fullest possibilities?

Why does what looked like paradise to you when viewed through youth's telescope now seem but a dreary desert? Because your vision is distorted. You are looking at your environment from a wrong point of view. You are disappointed, discontented and unhappy, because arriving where you are today, you have not found the fabled pot of gold at the foot of the rainbow. And so, disheartened, you bemoan your fate and squander your time—time that, properly used, could convert your present seeming desert into the very paradise of your early dreams.

We cannot separate our lives from time. Why is it that we are so extravagant, so thoughtless, in our waste of time, especially in youth, when we wish to cling so tenaciously to life? You cannot separate a wasted hour from the same duration of your life. If you waste your time, you must waste your life. If you improve your time, you cannot help improving your life.

How few people ever see the identity between their life and time! They seem to think they can waste time in all sorts of foolish ways, and even in dissipation, without wasting the life; but the two are inseparable. Remember, that when you throw away an evening or a day, or do infinitely worse than throw it away by indulging in pleasures which demoralize and tend to deteriorate your character and to form vicious habits, you are deliberately flinging away a part of your very life, and that when you grow old you will give anything to redeem the precious time you have squandered.

The reason many of our lives are so lean and poverty-stricken, so disappointing and ineffective, is that we do not really live in the day; we do not concentrate our energy, our ambition, our attention, our enthusiasm, upon the day we are living.

There is only one way really to live, and that is to start out every morning with a firm resolution to get the most out of that day, to live it to the full. No matter what happens or does not happen, what comes or does not come, resolve that you will extract from every experience of the day something of good, something that will make you wiser and show you how to make fewer mistakes tomorrow. Say to yourself, "This day I begin a new life. I will forget everything in the past that caused me pain, grief, or disgrace."

Resolve every morning that you will get the most out of *this* day, not of some day in the future when you are better off, when you have a family, when your children are grown up, when you have overcome your difficulties. *You never will overcome them all.* You will never be able to eliminate all the things which annoy, trouble, and cause friction in your life. You will never get rid of all the little enemies of your happiness, the hundred and one little annoyances, but *you can make the most of things as they are.*

It is not enough to extract happiness from ideal conditions. Anyone can do that. It is the self-mastered, the self-poised soul who can get happiness out of the most inhospitable surroundings. "Paradise is here or nowhere. You must take your joy with you or you will never find it."

The trouble with us is that we put too much emphasis on great happenings, the unusual things, and we overlook the common flowers on the path of life, from which we might abstract sweets, comforts, delights. Those alone are happy who have learned to extract happiness not from ideal conditions, but from the actual ones about them. Those who have mastered this secret will not wait for ideal surroundings; they will not wait until the next year, next decade, until they become rich, until they can travel abroad, until then ca afford to surround themselves with works of the great masters. They will make the most out of life today—right where they are.

I once knew a mother from whom death had taken away every one of her children, her husband and nearly all her relatives. Her circumstances were any thing but ideal. She prayed that death might now relieve her from her awful suffering. But she found a way to overcome her seemingly bleak circumstances, to turn a desert into a land of milk and hone. She realized that in having suffered so much, she had leaned from suffering how to console others. Soon, she was cheerful and happy again. The world did not seem so black and life such a failure as she thought it would be. There were too many who needed her mothering.

Resolve to enjoy yourself today. Enjoy *today*, and do not let the hideous shadows of tomorrow, the forebodings, and the things you dread, rob you of what is yours today your inalienable right to be happy *today*.

Just have a little heart-to-heart talk with yourself every morning, and say: "It does not matter what comes or what goes today, what happens or what does not happen, there is one thing of which I am sure, and that is, I am going to get the most possible out of the day. I am not going to allow anything to rob me of my happiness, or of my right to *live this day from begin to end*, and not merely to exist.

"I do not care what comes, I shall not allow any annoyance, any happening, any circumstances which may cross my path today, to rob me of my peace of mind. I will not be unhappy today, no matter what occurs. I am going to enjoy the day to its full, live the day completely. This day shall be a complete day in my life. I shall not allow the enemies of my happiness to mar it. No misfortune in the past, nothing which has happened to me in days gone by, which has been disagreeable or tragic, no enemies of my happiness or efficiency, shall be a guest in my spirit's sacred enclosure today. Only happy thoughts, joy thoughts, only the friends of my peace, comfort, happiness, and success, shall find entertainment in my soul this day. None of my enemies shall gain admittance to scrawl their hideous autographs on the walls of my mind. There shall be *'no admittance'* today, except to the friends of my best moods. I will tear down the black, sable pictures and hang pictures of joy, and gladness, of things which will encourage, cheer, and increase my power. Everything which ever handicapped my life, which has made me uncomfortable and unhappy, shall be expelled, at least for this day." So that when night comes I can say *"I have lived today."*

A clean, new, optimistic start like this, every morning, will very quickly revolutionize your outlook upon life and increase your power tremendously. It is just a question of mastering the brain, of forming new thought tracts in the soft brain tissue, making a path for a new happiness habit.

The great majority of people act as though the proper thing to do is to live almost anywhere except right *here* and *now*.

Start out every day with the tacit understanding with yourself that whatever comes or does not come, whether you are successful in your particular undertaking or unsuccessful, you will at least be happy as you go along—that you will not allow anything to rob you of the enjoyment which ought to come to you each day. Resolve that you will not allow any little accident or incident, or any conditions, however trying, to interrupt the natural flow of your sense of well-being, comfort, and happiness.

Remember that yesterday is dead. Tomorrow is not yet born. The only time that belongs to you is the passing moment. Resolutely build a wall about today and live within the enclosure. The past may have been hard, sad, or wrong—but it is over.

Liken the sixty minutes in the hour to one-of-a-kind flowers that only lives for sixty minutes and then die. If you do not savor those flowers now, they will never return for you to be able to do so.

Yes, a new flower will come in another hour, but only *this one* is available to enjoy now.

Today I will…

- *Be mindful—mindful of the pleasures that are right here and now around me; mindful of the little, as well as the grand, moments that bring me joy; mindful of the lives around me that are also trying to find some meaning in this life, in this very moment, and that I can give attention to, service to.*

- *Remember that the past is gone and the future is not yet—the opportunities of yesterday are gone; the words I wish I hadn't spoken have been spoken … but the regrets of yesterday as well as the happy memories now passed can be the lessons of today. As Wordsworth wrote, "Though nothing can bring back the hour, of splendour in the grass, of glory in the flower; we will grieve not, rather find strength in what remains behind."*

- *Remind myself that if I am not living in the today, then when will I live? If I am not extracting every moment of happiness from today, then from what moments will I extract happiness?*

- *Let go of yesterday. Every day is a new start. No matter how many mistakes, failures, etc., you have made in the past, today can be a new beginning. When Peter asked Jesus if he, Peter, should allow some to sin against him seven times yet still be forgiven, Jesus told him no, not seven times, but "seventy times seven." You, too, can forgive yourself "seventy times seven" times for whatever wrongs you believe you've done in the past and let go. Nobody is perfect; everyone has made mistakes. Today can be a new beginning.*

→ *Think of today as a flower that only blooms for twenty-four hours—I can savor it, inhaling every bit of its fragrance; I can offer it to another and share its beauty; or I can ignore it ... the choice is mine. How will you choose?*

→ _____
_____
→ _____
_____
→ _____
_____
→ _____
_____

chapter 16

TAKING LIFE TOO SERIOUSLY

*If a man insisted on always being serious, and
never allowed himself a bit of fun and relaxation,
he would go mad or become unstable without knowing it.*
—Herodotus

How quickly we Americans exhaust life! With what panting haste we pursue everything! It seems that practically everyone you meet appears to be late for an appointment. We have become like the Chinese sage who looked at an egg and expected "to hear it crow."

"I question if care and doubt ever wrote their names so legibly on the faces of any other population," said Emerson. "Old age begins in the nursery."

We take life much too seriously. We do not have half enough fun.

Look about you in your workplace and notice how many, as they look up and see the hours of the day ticking away and see the work they yet have to do, have a haunted, hounded look, as though they suspected either a policeman or a detective were on their trail. We are to often much too worried and anxious every minute. We take our vocations so very seriously, giving the impression that the whole universe is hanging upon the result of our tasks.

Even on the one day a week when many of us go to churches and temples, instead of hearing praise for the God who made the magnificent flowers, painted the butterflies, made all things beautiful in their time, what we hear a sermon is pitched in a minor key—discouraging and depressing; replete with the message of our faults, errors, shortcomings, and sins. The essence of faith is to uplift, encourage, and exalt—not to depress or deprecate. We all have burdens enough of our own to bear and do not need someone to further inject dark, doleful pictures in our minds.

"Away with these fellows who go howling through life," wrote Henry Ward Beecher, "and all the while passing for birds of paradise."

"Some people have an idea that they comfort the afflicted when they groan over them," says Talmage. "Don't drive a hearse through a man's soul."

Why take life so seriously, anyway? Play will not only improve your health, but increase your courage, determination, outlook, and efficiency wonderfully—heightening and multiplying them. It is an essential part of the shrewdest, most profitable business policy you can adopt.

Some of us are beginning to realize that we have taken life too seriously, that we have not had enough play in our lives, that we have not had half enough fun. If you are too absorbed in your business or vocation to hone your life and health with wholesome recreation, your are like a laborer who is too busy to sharpen his or her tools.

There is no greater delusion than that we can accomplish more by working a great many hours, straining mind and body to the limit of endurance. Great efficiency and vigorous mental concentration are impossible when the mind is over-strained, fatigued, or when we do not have sufficient recreation to restore its elasticity, its rebound. It is a pernicious and injurious fallacy to think that the more you work the more you will accomplish in life. The fact is that what we achieve in life depends upon the *effectiveness* of our work, upon the *efficiency* of if, rather than upon the length of time we spend at it. And it is in play as well as work that effectiveness and efficiency are developed. But in play, there is also the added and important element of recreation and diversion.

Where did the idea come from that we should take life so seriously, anyway? When and where did the serious people learn to say, "Keep away from me, life is too serious a matter to be spent on trivial things"? Why should we be such slaves to his bread winning? We ought to be able to get a good living, even to make fortunes, and yet have a good time every day of our lives. This idea of being a slave most of the time, and of only occasionally enjoying a holiday, is all wrong. Every day should be a holiday, a day of joy and gladness, a day of supreme happiness—and it would be, if we lived sanely, if we knew the secret of right thinking and normal living.

Why, even in the midst of our joys and pleasures, do so many of us entertain the notion that the famed Damocletian sword of pain hangs over us, held by the thinnest thread, ever ready to fall and pierce our moments happiness? Why do so many seem not to enjoy anything without the anticipation of some foreboding even that will soon shatter their pleasure? They, give the impression that they are conscious of some skeleton's presence at every feast.

Life is given us for enjoyment, not for one long, strenuous, straining Sisyphean struggle. Living-getting is intended to be only an incidental in the larger scheme of life.

It is impossible for any normal being to keep life in harmony without recreation and play. And the time spent in such moments need not be great in order to reap great benefits.

What magic even a single hour's fun will often work on a tired soul!

Have we not, indeed, all felt the wonderful balm, the great uplift, the rejuvenation which comes from just an hour of play time with family or friends after we have left a hard, exacting day's work and our bodies are jaded and we are brain weary and exhausted?

When you allow yourself time to have fun, you begin and end your day in better spirits, you are more hopeful, and you go to sleep at night happy—in a more contented frame of mind.

Take your fun every day as you go along. That is the only way to be sure of it. Do not postpone your happiness.

Remember, it is said that "the easy chair is a necessary part of the strenuous life."

Remember, too, that there is something else in the world more important than making money. At the end of your life, your health, your family, and your friendships will mean a thousand times more to you than the hours you took from them in the seriousness of dollar-chasing.

Today I will...

- *Find something humorous or to joke about about my problems, even though they may be very serious. Comedians find something to joke about about virtually every situation—national calamities, human foibles, their own problems in life, etc. When you hear them, you laugh. Pretend, then, that you're a comedian finding the humorous element, the joke, in your situation. There will always be time again to be serious later.*
- *Believe in my causes, but not express them so seriously that others find me overbearing. It's good to believe in something passionately; it's good to believe in something seriously. But we do not win the support or ear of others if they feel that when we speak, they are being browbeaten.*
- *Look for something to find cheerful, or joyful, or to laugh about in my various circumstances. There is something serious about work; there is even something serious about play. But there is nothing so serious that it can't be done better, more satisfyingly, more rewardingly, without moments of play.*
- *Remind myself that if everything I do I do seriously, then at the end of my day I might feel a sense of satisfaction, accomplishment—but I will not have had a moment of happiness.*

- _____
  _____
- _____
  _____
- _____
  _____
- _____
  _____

chapter 17

THE ALCHEMY OF A CHEERFUL MIND

*A merry heart maketh a cheerful countenance.
He that is of a merry heart hath a continual feast.*
—Proverbs: 15:13, 15

We typically avoid the company of those who are always grumbling, who are full of "ifs" and "buts" and "I told you so's"—who are ever complaining about their hard times, their hard lot. Instead, we gravitate toward those who can find the sun whether it shines or not.

"Wondrous is the strength of cheerfulness," said Carlyle, "altogether past calculation its powers of endurance. Efforts, to be permanently useful, must be uniformly joyous, a spirit all sunshine, graceful from very gladness, beautiful because bright."

It is despairing to go about with a face which indicates that life has been a disappointment to you instead of a glorious joy. And yet, some people have a genius for seeing only the crooked, the evil, and disagreeable. The have a faculty for touching the wrong keys. From the finest instrument they extract only discord. They sound the note of pessimism everywhere. All their songs are in a minor key. Everything is looking down. The shadows predominate in all their pictures: There is nothing bright, cheerful, or beautiful about them. Their outlook is always gloomy: times are always hard and money is always tight. Everything in them seems to be contracting; nothing expanding or growing or widening in their lives.

Take two persons just home from a vacation. "One has positively seen nothing, and has always been robbed: the landlady was a harpy, the bedroom was unhealthy, and the mutton was tough. The other has always found the cosiest nooks, the cheapest houses, the best landladies, the finest views, and the best dinners."

Give me someone like the deacon who was always noted for expressing his gratitude in the prayer meetings for some special blessing. He seemed just as cheerful and optimistic as ever, even though all sorts of misfortunes and hard luck had followed him all his life, and he had lost everything he had ever had—every member of his family, his home, his property, his health. His friends wondered what he could find to be grateful for. "Waal," he said, "even if I've lost everything in the world, I'm still thanking the Lord I've two teeth left—and one opposite t'other."

People such as this, who have learned to surround themselves with an atmosphere of peace and harmony, no matter what discord and darkness are in their environment, are those who have learned the last lesson of culture.

And how glad we all are to welcome sunny souls! We are never too busy to see them. There is nothing we welcome so much as sunshine.

"The cheerful heart makes its own blue sky," it is said. And how true! We all know how the day seems to rejoice with us when we are cheerful. The very sun and the flowers seem to reflect our joy. And then, when we are melancholy and blue, all nature takes on the same expression—while, of course, there is no real change in nature, yet to us this apparent change is tremendous.

Emerson says, "Do not hang a dismal picture on your wall, and do not deal with sables and glooms in your conversation."

We were not made to express discord, but harmony; to express beauty, truth, love, and happiness; wholeness, not halfness; completeness, not incompleteness. The mental temple was not given us for the storing of things that distress us. It was intended for the abode of the gods, for the treasuring of high purposes, grand aims, noble aspirations.

Refuse to be gloomy. Cheer up! Get your mind off your troubles. Do not think about them. Think of the bright things in life. It takes only a drop of oil to stop a screeching axle or hinge. In like manner, just a little bit of sunshine scatters the shadows.

Think gratefully of the good things you have, and be cheerful. No matter what pitfalls seem to loom before you—what poverty, what misfortune—keep in mind that no one has truly begun to fail until that person has lost his or her cheerfulness, the optimistic outlook upon life. It is only when we carry about a gloomy face that we then advertise the fact that hope has died out of us; that life has been a disappointment.

What a marvelous gift to have that mental alchemy which makes even poverty seem palatable, or which sees the ludicrous side of misfortune It is, after all, easy to be bright and optimistic when one enjoys robust health and is prosperous, but it requires heroic qualities to be so when poor health mocks ambition, and we are surrounded by disheartening conditions.

Develop the ability to get on with scolding, irritating people. To preserve serenity in the presence of those who think it their God-given duty to identify faults and straighten others out is a happy gift. The test of character is one's ability to remain cheerful, serene, hopeful, even under fire.

A man who was offended by a pungent newspaper article, the office of the New York *Tribune* and inquired for the editor. He was shown into a little seven-by-nine sanctum, where Horace Greeley sat, with his head close down to his paper, scribbling away. The angry man began by asking if this was Mr. Greeley. "Yes, sir; what do you want?" said the editor quickly, without once looking up from his paper. The irate visitor then began using his tongue, with no reference to the rules of propriety, good breeding, or reason. Meantime Mr. Greeley continued to write. Page after page was dashed off in the most impetuous style, with no change of features, and without paying the slightest attention to the visitor. Finally, after, about twenty minutes of the most impassioned scolding ever poured out in an editor's office, the angry man became disgusted, and abruptly turned to walk out of the room. Then, for the first time, Mr: Greeley quickly looked up, rose from his chair, and, slapping the gentleman familiarly on his shoulder, in a pleasant tone of voice said: "Don't go, friend; sit down, sit down, and free your mind; it will do you good—you will feel better for it. Besides, it helps me to think what I am to write about. Don't go."

Do you go through life wretched, miserable, or do yo rise about the petty annoyances which destroy the peace of so many people? Learn the fine art of enjoying everybody and everything. Like the bee, get honey from everywhere. Form the habit of getting good out of every experience. You can get something which will enrich your life, something helpful, out of everybody you meet. Every experience has something which would help somebody. Why not you?

A business woman, for example, tells of this interesting experiment she made:

"I started out to my work one morning, determined to try the power of cheerful thinking (I had been moody, sullen, and discouraged long enough). I said to myself: 'I have often observed that a happy state of mind has a wonderful effect upon my physical make-up, so I will try its effect upon others, and see if my right thinking can be brought to act upon them.' You see I was curious. As I walked along, more and more resolved on my purpose, and persisting that I was happy, that the world was treating me well, I was surprised to find myself lifted up, as it were; my carriage became more erect, my step lighter, and I had the sensation of treading on air. Unconsciously, I was smiling, for I caught myself in the act once or twice. I looked into the faces of the women I passed and there saw so much trouble and anxiety, discontent, even to peevishness, that my heart went out to them, and I wished I could impart to them a wee bit of the sunshine I felt pervading me.

"Arriving at the office, I greeted the bookkeeper with some passing remark, that for the life of me I could not have made under different conditions; I am not naturally witty; it immediately put us on a pleasant footing for the day; *she* had caught the reflection. The president of the company was a very busy man and much worried over his affairs, and at some remark that he made about my work I would ordinarily have felt quite hurt (being too sensitive by nature and education); but this day I had determined nothing should mar its brightness, so replied to him cheerfully. His brow cleared, and there was another pleasant footing established, and so throughout the day I went, allowing no cloud to spoil its beauty for me or others about me. At the kind home where I was staying the same course was pursued, and, where before I had felt estrangement and want of sympathy, I found congeniality and warm friendship. People will meet you halfway if you will take the trouble to go that far.

"So, if you think the world is not treating you kindly, don't delay a day, but say to yourself: 'Even if things do not always come my way, I am going to live for others and shed sunshine across the pathway of all I meet.' You will find happiness springing up like flowers around you, will never want for friends or companionship. And, above all the peace of God will rest upon your soul."

There is no habit which will give more satisfaction than to develop a happy alchemy. It will turns prose to poetry, ugliness to beauty, discord to melody. There are fewer hearts hungering for money than are hungering for love and sympathy and cheer—and with a happy alchemy, these you can always give.

"Happiness, laughter, and cheer!" someone wrote. "Scatter them wherever you go like roses on your path. Give them in place of grudges and throw them out instead of hints. Exchange them for insinuations and substitute them for complaints. Take them to your shopmates in the morning and bring them back to your loved ones at noon. Bestow them in the office and send them in the mail. Carry them to the sick and leave them with the unconsoled. Everywhere and always, warm up the cold streets and hearthstones of the world."

A cheerful disposition that scorns every rebuff of fortune and laughs in the face of disaster is a divine gift. "Fate itself has to concede a great many things to the cheerful man."

To be able to laugh away trouble is greater fortune than to possess the mines of King Solomon.

And it is a fortune that is within the reach of us all.

Today I will…

→ *Take joy with me; cling to her, no matter where I go or what I do. Cheerfulness is the analgesic balm that will soften the sorrows of life.*

→ *Adopt the sun-dial's motto: "I record none but hours of sunshine."*

- *Remind myself that the good excludes the bad; that the higher always shuts out the lower; that the greater motive and the grander affection, excludes the lesser, the lower; that the good is more than a match for the bad.*
- *Remember that every experience has something which can help somebody—why not me? This is not to say that every experience is pleasant, but that you can learn something from every situation that will teach you something about pleasantness—and your opportunity to experience it.*
- *Stop for a moment in front my bathroom or bedroom mirror this morning and remind myself that the person I'm looking at is the only one who can keep me from being cheerful today.*

- _____
  _____
- _____
  _____
- _____
  _____
- _____
  _____

chapter 18

TAKE A PLEASANT THOUGHT TO BED WITH YOU

I will both lay me down in peace, and sleep.
—Psalms 4:8

Many people lie down to sleep as the camels lie down in the desert, with their packs still on their backs They do not seem to know how to lay down their burdens: their minds go on working a large part of the night. If you are inclined to worry during the night, to keep your mental faculties on the strain, taut, it will be a good plan for you to have a bow in your bedroom and unstring it every night as a reminder that you should also unstring your mind so that it will not lose its springing power. The Indian knows enough to unstring his bow just as soon as he uses it so that it will not lose its resilience.

If you work hard all day and use your brain a large part of the night, doing your work over and over again, you cannot help but get up in the morning weary, jaded. Instead of having a clear, vigorous brain capable of powerfully focusing your mind, you will be approaching your work with all your standards down—and with about as much chance of winning as would a horse who has been driven all night before a race.

It is of the utmost importance to stop the grinding, rasping process in the brain at night and to keep from wearing life away and wasting your precious vitality.

Many people become slaves to night worry. They get into a chronic habit of thinking after they retire—especially of contemplating their troubles and trials—and it is a very difficult habit to break. They suffer so much torture at night that they actually dread to retire because of the long, tedious, wakeful hours. They use up almost as much mental energy in a restless night as during their actual work in the day.

Financial troubles in particular become exaggerated at night, as the imagination is particularly active at night. All unpleasant, disagreeable things can seem a great deal worse *then* than in the day, because in the silence and darkness, imagination magnifies everything. At night, even many optimists suffer more or less from pessimism then.

It is fundamental to sound health to make it a rule never to discuss business troubles and things that vex and irritate one at night just before retiring, for whatever is dominant in the mind when you fall asleep continues its influence on your nervous structure long into the night.

Have we not all at one time or another gone to sleep and dreamed of some experience from the past evening? Perhaps it is the refrain of a song or the intense situation in a play or movie that we saw that we live over again. This shows how powerful impressions are; how important it is never to retire to rest in a fit of temper or in an ugly, unpleasant mood. Mental discord saps vitality, lessens courage, shortens life. It does not pay to indulge in violent temper, corroding thoughts, mental discord in any form. Life is too short, too precious, to spend any part of it in such unprofitable, soul-racking, health-destroying business.

We should get ourselves into mental harmony, should become serene and quiet before retiring, and, if possible, lie down smiling, no matter how long it may take to secure this condition.

We must remind ourselves to turn off our brain power at the end of the day—just as we would not think of leaving our offices at the end of the work day without turning off the machinery. Or of turning off all the lights in our homes before retiring.

Why carry your business home, take it to bed with you, and waste your life forces? Even if you do manage to go to sleep with such a troubled mind, the brain keeps on working and you will wake up exhausted. Shut off your mental steam when you quit work. Lock up your business when you lock up your office or factory at night. Don't drag it into your home to mar your evening or to distress your sleep.

Some people age more at night than during the daytime, when, we would think the reverse would be true. When hard at work during the day, they do not have much time to think of their ailments, their personal or business troubles, their misfortunes. But when they retire, the whole brood of troubling thoughts and worry ghosts fill their minds with horrors. They grow older instead of younger—which they would were they under the influence of sound, refreshing sleep.

Never retire with a frown on your brow; with a perplexed, troubled, vexed expression. Smooth out the wrinkles; drive away all the enemies of your peace of mind, and never allow yourself to go to sleep with critical, cruel, jealous thoughts toward anyone.

It is bad enough to feel inimical toward others when in their presence and under severe provocation or in a hot temper in their presence. You certainly cannot afford to continue this state of mind after the provocation has ceased. The wear and tear upon your nervous system and your health will take too much out of you.

Be at peace with all the world at least once every twenty-four hours. You cannot afford to allow the enemies of your happiness to etch their miserable images deeper and deeper into your life and character as you sleep

It is a great thing to form a habit of forgetting and forgiving before going to sleep, of clearing the mind of all happiness and success enemies. If you wish to wake up feeling refreshed and renewed, you simply must retire in a happy, forgiving, cheerful mood.

If you have been impulsive, foolish, or unkind during the day in your treatment of others; if you have been holding a vicious, ugly, revengeful, jealous attitude toward others, the night is a good time to wipe off the slate and start anew. It is a blessed thing to put into practice St Paul's exhortation to the Ephesians: "Let not the sun go down upon your wrath."

If you have a grudge against another, forget it, wipe it out, erase it completely, and substitute a charitable love thought, a kindly, generous thought, before you fall asleep.

Clean your mental house before retiring. Throw out everything that causes you pain, everything that is disagreeable, undesirable; all unkind thoughts of anger, hatred, jealousy, all selfish, uncharitable thoughts. Do not allow them to print their hideous pictures upon your mind.

Then, when you have let go of all the rubbish and have swept and dusted and garnished your mind, fill it full of the pleasantest, sweetest, happiest, most helpful, encouraging, uplifting thought-pictures possible. Give yourself an evening happiness-bath. That ought to be the custom of everyone. A bath of love and good-will toward every living creature is more important than a water bath.

Make a habit of clearing the your mind every night of its enemies, of driving them all out before you go to sleep, your slumber will be undisturbed by hideous dreams and you will rise refreshed, renewed.

No matter how tired or busy you are, or how late you retire, make it a rule never to go to sleep without erasing every unfortunate impression, every disagreeable experience, every unkind thought, every particle of envy, jealousy, and selfishness, from the mind. *Just imagine that the words "harmony," "good cheer," and "good will to every living creature" are written all over your bedroom in letters of light.*

If you have any difficulty in banishing unpleasant or torturing thoughts, force yourself to read some good, inspiring book—something that will smooth out your wrinkles and put you in a happy mood; something that will make you see the real grandeur and beauty of life; something that will make you feel ashamed of petty meannesses and narrow, uncharitable thoughts.

After a little practice, you will be surprised to see how quickly and completely you can change your whole mental attitude so that you will face life the right way before you fall asleep.

You will be surprised also to find how wonderfully serene, calm, refreshed, and rejuvenated you will be when you wake in the morning, and how much easier it will be to start right, and wear a smile that won't come off during the day, than it was when you went to bed in an ill-humored, worrying, or ugly mood—or full of ungenerous; uncharitable thoughts.

People who have learned the art of putting themselves into harmony with all the world before they retire, of never harboring a thought of jealousy, hatred, envy, revenge, or ill-will of any kind against any human being, get a great deal more out of sleep and retain their youth much longer and are much more efficient than those who have the habit of reviewing their disagreeable experiences and thinking about all their troubles and trials in the night.

Many have had their lives completely revolutionized by this experiment of putting themselves in tune before going to sleep. Formerly they were in the habit of retiring in a bad mood; tired, discouraged over anticipated evils and all sorts of worries and anxieties. They would worry over the bad things in their business, the unfortunate conditions and mistakes in their lives—and they would discuss their misfortunes in the late hours of night with their spouses. The result was that their minds were in an upset condition when they fell asleep, and these melancholy; ugly pictures—exaggerated in awful vividness in the stillness—became etched deeper and deeper into their minds, and they awoke in the morning weary and exhausted, instead of feeling, as every one should, like a newly-made creature with fresh ambition and invigorated determination.

Form the habit of making a call upon the Great Within of you before retiring. Gently ask it for guidance in self-betterment, self-enlargement, in patience, in wisdom—in the things you yearn for and long to realize but do not know how to bring about. Registering this request for something higher and nobler from your subconsciousness, *putting it right up to yourself*, will work like a leaven during the night. After a while all the building forces within you will help to unite in furthering your aim; in helping you to realize your vision.

There are marvelous possibilities for success building and happiness building in preparing your mind before going to sleep—in declaring, impressing upon your mind, and picturing as vividly as possible your ideals for yourself: what you would like to become and what you long to accomplish. Do this every night, instead of going to be fretting and worrying over things you can't undo or fix in that moment, and you will be surprised to see how quickly that wonderful force in your subjective self will begin to give shape to the pattern—to copy the model—which you have given it. In the great, interior, creative, restorative force of your subjective self lies the great secret of life. And blessed are those who find it.

But ultimately, the key is that we should fall asleep in the most cheerful, the happiest possible frame of mind. Our minds should be filled with lofty thoughts—with thoughts of love and of helpfulness—thoughts which will continue to create that which is helpful and uplifting, which will renew the soul and help us to awake in the morning refreshed and in superb condition for the day's work.

"Thou hast been called, O Sleep! The friend of woe," wrote the poet Robert Southey, "but 'tis the happy that call thee so."

The best preparation for a good night's sleep, then, the most assured way to take a pleasant thought to bed with you each night, is to spend as much of your day as you can in happiness.

Today I will…

→ *Refresh, renew, rejuvenate myself in the evening with play and pleasant recreation. Play as hard as you work; have a good time. Then you will get that refreshing, invigorating sleep which gives a surplus of energy and a buoyancy of spirit which will make you eager to plunge into tomorrow's activities.*

→ *If beset by troubling thoughts before I go to sleep, calm myself. Turn off your lights and focus your attention on your breath. Just listen to it. If troubling thoughts keep intruding, replace them by occupying your mind with non-troubling thoughts. For example, on each in breath, say to yourself (silently or out loud—but gently) "In," and on each out breath say "Out." Or say "One" on your in breath and "Two" on your out breath, continuing counting until you reach ten— then start with "One" again. Or purchase a recording of adagio music and play it as you lie in the darkness in bed. (Listening with earphones may even be better, especially if you live with someone who is lying in bed next to you. If you fall asleep with the earphones on, don't worry. Either you'll sleep through the night—which is what you want—or you'll wake up, remove them, and be able to return right back to sleep, because the music has been playing in your subconscious while you were sleeping. If it's an audiotape that you purchase, set your player to auto-reverse, so the tape automatically plays the second side. You might even want to set your player to "repeat," so the recording continues playing.)*

→ *Remind myself that the best way to get a good night's sleep is to prepare myself for a good night's sleep. Do everything you can to remove any concerns that might crop up as you're going to sleep. Early in the evening, write a list of all the things you have to do the next day. This should even include resuming a conversation with someone at work that was left unsettled and unsatisfying at the end of the day—with the understanding that you wish to resume the conversation calmly and with the intent of doing your part to resolve the disagreement. Early in the evening, forgive all the people who you feel have wronged you—and forgive yourself for anything you did that embarrassed, humiliated, disappointed, etc. you during the day. If you and a friend or loved one had a disagreement, work together on resolving it early in the night. Set out the clothes that you'll wear for the next day, if you wish. Place anything that you need to bring to work or do on a table beside your front door, so you wont have to go scurrying around for those things in the morning, or worry concern yourself about them before you go to bed. The idea is to rid yourself early in the evening of anything that might cause you to go to bed restless, preoccupied. Work out all the vexing things, and then having done so, let go of them at least an hour or so before going to bed. Then listen to calming music, read an entertaining book or newspaper/magazine article. In other words, begin relaxing.*

→ *Remind myself that ultimately, the best antidote to a restless night is happiness in my day.*

chapter 19

OPTIMISM

*'Twixt the optimist and the pessimist
The difference is droll:
The optimist sees the doughnut
But the pessimist sees the hole.*
—McLandburgh Wilson

It is related that Dwight L. Moody once offered his Northfield pupils a prize of five hundred dollars for the best thought. This took the prize: "Men grumble because God put thorns on roses; wouldn't it be better to thank God that He put roses with thorns?"

Optimism is a grand creed. You can adopt no better life philosophy. There is no other one thing that will contribute so much to the life that is worth while as the optimistic habit. The habit of carrying a cheerful, hopeful outlook, of looking for the best in your work, the best in everybody and everything is of untold value. It lights up one's pathway.

We win half the battle when we make up our minds to take the world as we find it, including the thorns.

"What is an optimist?" asked a farmer's boy.

"Well, John," replied his father, "you know I can't give ye the dictionary meanin' of that word any more'n I can of a great many others. But I've got a kind of an idee what it means. Probably you don't remember your Uncle Henry; but I guess if there ever was an optimist, he was one. Things was always coming out right with Henry, and especially anything hard that he had to do; it wasn't a-goin' to be hard—'twas jest sort of solid-pleasant.

"Take hoein' corn, now. If anything ever tuckered me out, 'twas hoein' corn in the hot sun. But in the field, 'long about the time I begun to lag back a little, Henry he'd look up an' say:

"'Good, Jim! When we get these two rows hoed, an' eighteen more, the piece'll be half done.' An' he'd say it in such a kind of a cheerful way that I couldn't 'a' ben any more tickled if the piece had been all done—an' the rest would go light enough.

"But the worst thing we had to do—hoein' corn was a picnic to it—was pickin' stones. There was no end to that on our old farm, if we wanted to raise anything. When we wa'n't hurried and pressed with somethin' else, there was always pickin' stones to do; an' there wa'n't a plowin' but what brought up a fresh crop, an' seems as if the pickin' had all to be done over again.

"Well, you'd 'a' thought, to hear Henry, that there wa'n't any fun in the world like pickin' stones. He looked at it in a different way from anybody I ever see. Once, when the corn was all hoed, and the grass wa'n't fit to cut yet, an' I'd got all laid out to go fishin', and father he up and set us to pickin' stones up on the west piece, an' I was about ready to cry, Henry he says,

"'Come on, Jim. I know where there's lots of nuggets.'

"An' what do you s'pose, now? That boy had a kind of a game that that there field was what he called a plasser mining field; and he got me into it, and I could 'a' sworn I was in Californy all day—we had such a good time.

"'Only,' says Henry, after we'd got through the day's work, 'the way you get rich with these nuggets is to get rid of 'em, instead of keepin 'em.'

"That somehow didn't strike my fancy, we'd had play instead of work, anyway, an' a great lot of stones had been rooted out of that field.

"An', as I said before, I can't give ye any dictionary definition of optimism; but if your Uncle Henry wa'n't an optimist, I don't know what one is."

An optimistic mind is a prism which brings the rainbow colors out of things which otherwise look ordinary.

"To one man," says Schopenhauer, "the world is barren, dull, and superficial; to another, rich, interesting, and full of meaning."

Take two persons just home from a vacation. "One has positively seen nothing, and has always been robbed: the landlady was a harpy, the bedroom was unhealthy, and the mutton was tough. The other has always found the cosiest nooks, the cheapest houses, the best landladies, the finest vies, and the best dinners."

We need more joy peddlers, and sunshine makers, more people who refuse to see the ugly, the bitter, and the crooked; who see a spark of beauty in the world, rather than the glow of discord.

What riches live in a sunny soul!

To do the maximum of which you are capable, keep your mind filled with sunshine—with beauty and truth, with cheerful, uplifting thoughts. Bury everything that makes you unhappy and discordant, everything that cramps your freedom, that worries you—before it buries you.

Try the cultivation of the sunny side of your nature for a year. It will revolutionize your whole life. You will attract where now you repel; warm and cheer where now, perhaps, you chill and discourage. Compare the power of a shadow with that of a ray of sunlight. All the life, all the physical force on the globe, is in the stored up energy of the sunbeam. There is no life or hope in the darkness.

The first prize at a flower-show was taken by a pale, sickly little girl, who lived in a close, dark court in the east of London. The judges asked how she could grow the flower in such a dingy and sunless place. She replied that a little ray of sunlight came into the court; as soon as it appeared in the morning she put her flower beneath it, and, as it moved, moved the flower, that she kept it in the sunlight all day.

But it is those who see the world all its beauty, its sunshine, its promise, its hope, who have lifted civilization up from barbarity to its present condition. They scatter serenity and hope do more to lift the burdens of the world than the thousand long-faced, sober people who tell you to prepare for the world to come, but never have a smile for the world they are, in.

The bright, joyous heart is a great boon; the face that carries habitual sunshine a perpetual blessing.

Some people live in dungeons of their own making and then complain of the darkness and the gloom. But it is we who make the world we live in and shape our own environment.

The world we live in is the one that is reflected from within us. The whole world is but a whispering gallery, an echoing hall, which flings back the echo of our own complaints or commendations; a mirror which reflects the face we present to it.

Ask yourself: "What face am I presenting to the world today?"

The answer you give will make all the difference as to whether in this day you see the reflection of sorrow or of happiness.

Today I will...

→ *Be an optimist all day long. We commonly denigrate optimists as naive people who are wearing rose-colored glasses. But step in the shoes of an optimist for a day. Greet every experience with optimism, with an enthusiastic outlook of hope. See if at the end of the day, the world doesn't seem a little bit brighter to you than it has before. Then decide through which glasses you want to look at the world in the future: those of the optimist, or something more akin to them, or the ones you've been wearing previously.*

→ *Examine some of the phrases I use to see if they take the dim view of things. We give voice to many familiar expressions without realizing how they may be predisposing us to see the worst. We say, for example, that trouble comes in threes. But why can't joys come in threes as well? We say "It never rains but that it pours." Why don't we say, "It never rains but that somewhere a flower begins to grow"? Play with many of negative expressions in our language and turn them into positive ones. You might be surprised at how many negative ways we unwittingly speak about the world and ourselves. You may also be surprised at the way the world you've always known springs up anew when you turn a negative expression into a positive one.*

→ *Take a task I dread, that I've been putting off, and turn it into an adventure. Perhaps you've been putting off cleaning the garage in your home, or your home office, or your desk at your workplace, because it seems like such an overwhelming and laborious task. If it's your desk that your cleaning, pretend that somewhere in the pile of papers you have to sort through and decide whether to file, and where, or throw out, there's a sizable check for you that you accidentally misplaced and forgot about. (When you finish cleaning your desk and that imagined check doesn't turn up after all, don't abandon your sense of play. Open your checkbook and say, "Oh, it was here, after all, and not in all those papers!" Then write yourself a check for a treat of a pizza dinner—or whatever would be a treat at the end of a day of cleaning—for that night.)*

→ _____
  _____

→ _____
  _____

→ _____
  _____

→ _____
  _____

chapter 20

THE POWER OF HOME JOY

Over the roofs of the village
Columns of pale blue smoke, like clouds of incense ascending,
Rose from a hundred hearths, the homes of peace and contentment.
* * *
There the richest was poor, and the poorest lived in abundance.
—Longfellow

As it is with happiness, so too is it with a home: one doesn't need money to acquire the satisfaction of either. Gold can buy and furnish *houses*, but no money ever yet bought or made a *home*. It is the wealth of tenderness, of self-sacrifice, of kindliness, of peace that transforms the construction of mere brick and mortar into buildings we call houses into dwellings that are treasure-houses of the heart.

Some of the happiest homes I have ever known, ideal homes, where intelligence, peace, and harmony dwell, have been homes of poor people. No rich carpets covered the floors; there were no costly paintings on the walls, no piano, no library, no works of art. But there were contented minds, devoted and unselfish lives, each contributing as much as possible to the happiness of all, and endeavoring to compensate by intelligence and kindness for the poverty of their surroundings.

The important work that is done to turn a house into a home, then, is not done on the outside, but within. It is not on the outside—the well-trimmed lawn, the elegant architecture, the richly colored paint, the luxurious cars in the driveway—that a house becomes a home. These give only the appearance of wealth, not necessarily of harmonious home life. It is what is done within the walls of a house that turns that fine building into a home—and yet sadly there is where much is often lacking, and the opulent exterior is found to only be a veneer.

A judge of large experience, for instance, said that one of the chief grievances of women who come to him for relief through divorce is that their husbands neglect them and their homes for business, giving their minds so completely to office affairs that even when at home they are only surly brutes with whom the angels themselves could not lead happy domestic lives.

Working husbands and wives, do not bring your business troubles home with you!

We all know people who are agreeable and cheerful at the workplace but who become cross and intolerably disagreeable the moment they get home. They seem to think that they have license to vent their spleen in the home, as it belongs to them. If any one has injured them during the day, they seem to try to get even by maltreating members of their own family. They reserve their sunshine for the outside world, and carry their gloom, their sadness, and their melancholy home for family consumption. Their home-coming is dreaded as a disturbing element.

How many people thwart their own home life by turning a smiling face to the world, and a sour, faultfinding one to their homes! They have managed to be half decent during the day, because so many eyes were watching them: their pride and vanity kept them from making a fool of themselves before others. But then, when they get home, they ask themselves Why shouldn't they throw off their restraint and do what they feel like doing?—making a kicking post of the home.

Think of those who come home and snarl at the person they love. They enter with a growl for a greeting, pushing the spouse or children out of the way, and taking refuge as soon as possible behind a book or paper or some other form of distraction and entertainment. Then these same people wonder why their homes are not more agreeable, why their spouses do not think more of them, why their children do not run to meet them with joy and gladness.

You must bring sunshine home with you if you expect it to be reflected back to you. The joys of home come from giving and taking: they cannot be all one-sided. You cannot expect to get sunshine in return for gloom, despondency, irritability, and crabbedness. The rate of exchange is not that way. Your home is an investment, and you will get back in kind just what you put into it, with plenty of interest. If your investment is mean stingy, and contemptible, you cannot expect to draw large dividends of sweetness, serenity repose, and happiness. A home is a bank of happiness. If you deposit counterfeit money, you cannot expect to draw out the genuine coin of social exchange. There is no way for you to get happiness out unless you put happiness-material into it.

Not only on account of your home, but also on your own account, you should not keep business in mind all the time. A bow that is always bent loses its elasticity, so that it will not send the arrow home with force when there is need. Those who think day and night about their business weaken their faculties and lose their buoyancy and "snap" by never allowing themselves a chance to become freshened, strengthened, and rejuvenated. What a pitiable sight to see a person piling up a big fortune with all their might and utterly neglecting the very thing for which we were all born: self-enlargement and happiness shared with another loving person, and where possible and desired, children.

My friend, if I have been describing you, ask yourself right now how much have you ever done to deserve the harmony, love and encouragement in the home that you seek and may not be receiving. If you are always bringing your work home with you, do you not wonder that your children, sensitive to your moods, prefer to play by themselves, or with other children, rather than being pushed away by you who never seems to have the time to show them affection, to play with them? Why they may scarcely know you except by a hurried "Good night" at the end of the day.

Keep in mind that no matter if your business affairs are not going just as you would have them, you are only wasting the energy and mental power—energy and power which would enable you to overcome these unfortunate conditions—by dragging your business into your home, and worrying and fretting and harming your family over circumstances that they could not help.

This does not mean, though, that you should not keep your spouse informed about your business. We should talk over our affairs with one another; our spouses should always know the exact conditions at our business. Many a person has come to grief by keeping his or her mate in ignorance of straitened circumstances or declining business, of the fact that he or she was temporarily pressed for capital and unable to indulge in certain luxuries. A loving partner can be of great help in offsetting your business concerns if he or she knows just how things are going and what is required from him or her to be of support. Your spouses contribution of personal and household economy and planning may give just the needed support you're seeking, the relief from your concerns. Moreover, his or her sympathy at just the right moment may take out the sting of pain that will enable you to bear your trials the following morning. This confiding frankly with one another is a great difference than the disagreeable feature of harping at one another because of your business stresses and strains, and letting your business concerns ruin your attitude toward your loved ones, making life miserable for those not to blame.

Better to fail in money-making than in home making. Commit yourself to making your home the place where both you and your loved one always long to go and are loath to part.

It is the grand secret of a happy home to express the affection you really have.

It should be the great aim of married people to keep the commonplace out of their lives and maintain not only love, but the expression of it in a hundred delicate, winning ways.

Once, upon being asked at a dinner party who he would prefer to be if he could not be himself, Joseph H. Choate, the American Minister at the Court of St. James, hesitated a moment, apparently running over in his mind the great ones on earth, when his eyes rested on Mrs. Choate at the other end of the table, who was watching him with great interest in her face, and suddenly he replied, "If I could not be myself, I should like to be Mrs. Choate's second husband."

With many, however, romance ends with the marriage—just as a hunter's interest dies with the game when he has fired the shot that kills. I have been in homes where one partner treated the other more as a servant or lowly employee, than as a companion. If one complained of a headache or of feeling unwell, the other never showed any sympathy, but on the contrary, appeared provoked, and often made sarcastic remarks.

Much of this change in temperament is occasioned by our sudden discovery that married life is different than we'd been led to believe. Lovers fondly fancy that they will never have a quarrel. The truth is that most husbands and wives have differences. But these need not be problems if the two are willing to learn to respect each other's differences, to remember the reasons they fell in love, and to accommodate and reconcile. This can be achieved if in the home they will follow one rule: never go to sleep at night except in friendly harmony. If there has been a disturbance of peace, settle it before bedtime. If either has done or said anything to wound the other, confess and seek forgiveness before the head touches the pillow. Resolve to never let the sun go down on your wrath.

"If you knew your marital partner would be dead a year from today, how would you conduct yourself for the next twelve months?" poignantly asks Ella Wheeler Wilcox.

"Would you lose your temper over trifles, and spoil your own and another's comfort because there was a late meal, or a mistake about the time or place you were to meet each other, and would you nag and irritate and antagonize the one you are bound to for life?

"I am sure you would not. You would be very considerate and patient and kind, knowing the face you looked upon was so soon to be hidden from your sight—the voice you listened to so soon to be stilled. You would think of all that man's or woman's virtues; you would recall all the early days of courtship, and you would make the same excuses for shortcomings you did in that romantic era.

"Why not use the same forbearance, affection, and courtesy toward the man or woman who is liable to live twenty years as toward one who is to die very soon? If people are properly mated, the real romance begins with marriage."

But is it not sad to see that in so many relationships, in so many homes, the woman sacrifices infinitely more for the man she loves than he does for her. Look at how many women stay in crushing relationships, in the hopes that one day the man in her life will see the love that is waiting there for him.

Men often think that they are superior to their wives because they earn more, as if it requires superior ability to earn money. As a fact, much of their success is due to the wife's influence, due to her tact within the home and outside at social functions, her ability to keep her husband in good working trim, to keep him from worrying or to be there to calm him when his mind is beset with worries and discouragements—all sorts of things which, but for her, might cripple his earning capacity and lower his efficiency.

Most men are much saner, much more normal and level-headed, economical and careful, on account of their wives. She develops the affectionate side of his nature and renders his character stronger and more symmetrical. Men should study to prevent early disappointments in their marriages, understanding that everyone one can produce very much more where there is harmony and affection.

I have known and know now many women who claim nothing and who get no credit from the world, who are, nonetheless, the real brains behind a statesman's reputation. And there are others who assist their husbands in such secrecy that the fact that they are helping is hidden, even from the husband,

Some one has said that "marriage is an episode in the life of a man, an epoch in the life of a woman." Many men are not so firmly attached to their wives by their affection as their wives are to them. A devoted wife is apt to overlook a man's weaknesses; he is often more selfishness, possessive, in his affection. And more often than not, when she gives her love it is for all time; her love is generally less selfish and her devotion is not as dependent upon the man's attractiveness as is his for her.

At the same time, it is true that many married women often make the fatal mistake of not making themselves attractive in every possible way after marriage as they did before. But often this is because there is no encouragement for her to fix herself up prettily for a man, who now takes her for granted, who never notices what she has on or how her hair is arranged, unless it be to criticize it unfavorably.

And is it not a common complaint of women that their husbands seldom truly *talk* to them? It is not easy for a woman to be bright and entertaining when she talks to a man who merely grunts or scowls in reply. Single-handed and alone she cannot make the home joy. Why should you speak to your wife in a tone of voice that you would not dare to use toward a woman at your place of work?

How many people do you know who are really happy? And yet, each human being is trying to be happy, really wants to be happy—most especially in choosing his or her marriage partner. But too often one hears discord instead of harmony in the home.

How many pangs we suffer, what humiliations, what embarrassments, simply from not expressing harmony. We did not want to pain those we love, to be irritable, fretful; we did not want to destroy the peace of our home; we did not want to injure the people we married; we had no idea of hurting them; we had no idea of reviling, criticizing, chastising, or abusing them when once we looked in that person's eyes and said "I will." But often we speak words that criticize and injure, and then that day we said "I will" seems so long ago.

When we lose command of our emotions we reveal the brute in ourselves—all the mean, contemptible, nasty disposition that we do everything in the world to conceal from our dearest friends and colleagues.

Just think what a revolution would come into our home lives if we were just more careful about the tone of our voices!

Notice how you can use the sweetest and most endearing words to a dog —and yet utter them in a tone of voice that will frighten him out of his wits and make him unhappy for hours. On the other hand, you can use the worst possible language, but convey it to him in a gentle, soothing voice—and bring him to you with set his tail wagging.

Much of the friction in life is caused by the tone of voice. The voice expresses our feelings, our attitude toward others. The discordant tone, which expresses antagonism and an uncongenial mental attitude, is trying.

Even the mechanical lowering of the voice, as you feel the hot blood rushing through your veins when angry, will tend to allay your passion. We know how angry children will work themselves up to a perfect rage by screaming and yelling when things go wrong. The louder they scream, the more they yell, the madder they get, until they sometimes become hysterical. Their own angry tone feeds the fire of passion; whereas, a low tone, a gentle tone would help to extinguish the brain fire.

How much unhappiness in the home would be avoided if all the members of the family could agree never to raise their voices! If fault-finding, censuring spouses would only instead read aloud in the magic book of endearing words to one another daily; if they would adopt in the married life the same methods as during courtship, when they were eager to win the object of their affection!

The sarcastic, cutting, resentful, discordant tone of voice is responsible for a large part of the unhappiness not only in the home, but also in business, and in society. It is the little disputes, little fault-findings, little insinuations, sharp criticisms, fretfulness and impatience, little unkindnesses, slurs, little discourtesies, bad temper, that create most of the discord and unhappiness in the family. How much it would add to the glory of our homes if it might be said of each of us what was said of Lord Holland's sunshiny face: "He always comes to breakfast like a man upon whom some sudden good fortune has fallen!"

People who are inclined to lose their temper, to fly into a passion at the slightest provocation, little realize that if they permit many of these conflagrations, the nerve cells will burn out the short circuits from constantly crossing the wires, injuring the fine, delicate mechanism of the brain, and after a while that they will lose the power of self-control, and be unable to restrain themselves. They will become hair-triggered and explode automatically.

There is no more humiliating spectacle than the exhibition of a person's meanest and most contemptible and most brutal qualities when in anger—and especially when in anger at a loved one. At such a time Reason is strangled. Wisdom hides her head in shame; Good Sense and Good Judgment get down off the throne; and the beast vaults upon the royal seat and Anarchy rules throughout the mental kingdom.

An after each partner has passed through such a passion fire, do they not feel that something precious has been burned out their lives? Your self-respect, your dignity, have been scorched in the conflagration.

I once saw a child in a perfect rage of passion taken before a mirror. He was so ashamed and chagrined at the awful spectacle that he stopped crying. If adults could only see themselves when they are burning up with passion, when the conflagration is raging through their brain, and tearing their nervous system to tatters, when the beast looks out of the eyes, it would seem as though they could never again be induced to make such spectacles of themselves.

If there is one thing we prize most it is harmony—physical and mental comfort. And the place we most envision as that source of harmony and permanent peace is the home. But a bad temper which is likely to explode at the slightest irritation is virtually as dangerous to that dream of peace and the safety of the household as the presence of gunpowder would be.

Each partner should try the praise plan, the appreciation plan for a while. Give up fault-finding.

"Praise is a heart stimulant. Blame is a heart depressant," says Dorothy Dix.

The value of pleasant words every day, as you go along, is well depicted by Aunt, Jerusha in what she said to our genial friend of *Zion's Herald*:

"If folk could have their funerals when they are alive and well and struggling along, what a help it would be!" she sighed, upon returning from a funeral, wondering how poor Mrs. Brown would have felt if she could have heard what the minister said. "Poor soul, she never dreamed they set so much by her!

"Mis' Brown got discouraged. Ye see, Deacon Brown, he'd got a way of blaming everything on to her. I don't suppose the deacon meant it—'twas just his way—but it's awful wearing. When things wore out or broke, he acted just as if Mis' Brown did it herself on purpose; and they all caught it, like the measles or the whooping-cough.

"And the minister a-telling how the deacon brought his young wife here when 'twa'n't nothing but a wilderness, and how patiently she bore hardship, and what a good wife she'd been! Now the minister wouldn't have known anything about that if the deacon hadn't told him. Dear! Dear! If he'd only told Mis' Brown herself what he thought, I do believe he might have saved the funeral.

"And when the minister said how the children would miss their mother, seemed as though they couldn't stand it, poor things!

"Well, I guess it is true enough—Mis' Brown was always doing for some of them. When they was singing about sweet rest in heaven, I couldn't help thinking that that was something Mis' Brown would have to get used to for she never had none of it here.

"She'd have been awful pleased with the flowers. They was pretty, and no mistake. Ye see, the deacon wa'n't never willing for her to have a flowerbed. He said 'twas enough prettier sight to see good cabbages a-growing; but Mis' Brown always kind of hankered after sweet-smelling things, like roses and such.

"What did you say, Levi? 'Most time for supper? Well, land's sake, so it is! I must have got to meditating. I've been a-thinking, Levi, you needn't tell the minister anything about me. If the pancakes and pumpkin pies are good, you just say so as we go along. It ain't best to keep everything laid up for funerals."

How true, then, are the following lines of the late Margaret Sangster:

If I had known in the morning
How wearily all the day
The words unkind would trouble my mind
That I said when you went away,
I had been more careful, darling,
Nor given you needless pain;
But we vex our own with look and tone
We may never take back again.

For though in the quiet evening
You may give me the kiss of peace,
Yet it well might be that never for me
The pain of the heart should cease!
How many go forth at morning,
Who never come home at night!
And hearts have broken for harsh words spoken,
That sorrow can ne'er set right.

We have careful thought for the stranger,
And smiles for the sometime guest;
But oft for "our own" the bitter tone,
Though we love our own the best.
Ah! lips with the curve impatient,
Ah! brow with the shade of scorn,
'Twere a cruel fate, were the night too late
To undo the work of the morn!

The majority of people do not realize how little it takes to make another happy. Most of us will put up with most everything—poverty and all sorts of hardships—but if the heart is not fed, we will wither and the best things will die out of us, even though we may live in a palace and be surrounded with regal luxuries.

"I noticed," said Franklin, "a mechanic among a number of others, at work on a house a little way from my office, who always appeared to be in merry humor; he had a kind word and smile for everyone he met. Let the day be ever so cold, gloomy, or sunless, a happy smile danced on his cheerful countenance. Meeting him one morning, I asked him to tell me the secret of his constant flow of spirits.

"'It is no secret, doctor,' he replied. 'I have got one of the best wives; and, when I go to work, she always has a kind word of encouragement for me; and when I go home, she meets me with a smile and a kiss; and then tea is sure to be ready; and she has done so many little things through the day to please me, that I cannot find it in my heart to speak an unkind word to anybody.'"

But sentiment and good cheer will not alone count for harmony in the home. There must also be practical adjustments—and in particular, with regard to the handling of money. Each person should try to avoid every possible means of friction, and there is no better way of avoiding a large part of it, than by forming an actual partnership with one another.

"… for there is nothing better than this," wrote Homer, "when a husband and wife keep a household in oneness of mind."

A great deal of the friction in the average home centers around financial matters. There is probably no one quality which is more misunderstood and abused in the home, as well as elsewhere, than economy. And a false economy is as fatal to the home joy as is lavishness to the individual.

There are many, in other words, who take scant pleasure in life because they are slaves to false economy and overwork. Saving becomes a fetish. Their economy is mean and stingy, even in their homes. They are always scolding about picayune wastes of life, cautioning everybody not to use too much of this or that, and making everybody about them miserable.

I have in mind a home where the atmosphere of poverty and denial predominates. The family does without even many of the comforts of life. False ideas of saving have so infected every member that it is positively painful to visit them. Only a little while ago I was at dinner in this house and the little boy of six remarked that they had mackerel that evening because they could get it cheaper than any other fish. Even the small children would ask the cost of things at the table when guests were present.

I know of another man who harps upon using too much butter and too much meat to such an extent that other members of the family fairly dread meal times. They dislike to put on a new pair of shoes or other articles of clothing because this man will make such a fuss and ask if their purchase was necessary.

One of the meanest traits is that of the stingy husband whose inclination is to exert a censorship over his wife's expenditures. It takes all the joy and interest out of her end of the partnership. If the wife happens to make a mistake in getting a bad bargain, many a man will get into a rage and make her miserable when perhaps he himself makes all sorts of foolish bargains, and takes home things which the wife knows are absolutely useless and that the money paid for them was practically thrown away.

I know a man who rarely ever asks his wife what she wants in the home, or, as he is working and she is home with their new baby, gives her money with which to buy things herself. He will buy furniture and bric-a-brac, all sorts of things at auctions and bargain sales which do, not match anything in the home, which are entirely out of place, and yet the wife does not dare to criticize her husband. He will buy a complete set of some author's works because he gets them cheap, when, perhaps there is not a single volume among them which any one in the home would care to read, and the wife knows perfectly well that a few selected volumes from choice authors would be worth than a whole library of such rubbish as the husband has brought home.

In other homes, multitudes of things are put away in attics and cupboards and closets which will never be used and which are a nuisance and ought to be burned up.

If only the husband is working, if the wife is taking care of the children and the home, then husbands should give their wives a certain proportion of the income every week or month, and to let them run the household as they see fit, and pay all the expenses without any question being asked as to where the money went. The wife pays the provision bills, buys the clothing for the family and pays her own personal expenses. No questions are asked. She will delight in her independence. Disputes are not as liable to arise as it is when money is doled out to the wife piecemeal. Moreover, the truth be known, as a rule, it is a very rare man who can spend money for the home so wisely and with as good taste as can the wife.

Many men allow their wives to wear themselves out in their early married life in order, they claim, to enable the household to save a little money and get a start in the world. But then, after the couple have become prosperous, many of those same men are ashamed of their wives, because through hard work and self-denial for false economy's sake, they have lost their attractiveness. Then many of these men conclude that they are not compatible, get a divorce, and marry some young, attractive girl who can shine in society.

At a reception not long ago, for example, I met a multimillionaire who had worked his way to the front from extreme poverty, and whose wife had sacrificed her beauty and all her grace of form and her charm in the terrible struggle to help him on his feet and practically out of bankruptcy in their younger days. She had a sweet face, but it was sad. There was character there, but almost a total lack of the charm which attracts selfish men.

The man himself was faultlessly dressed, splendidly groomed. He was so much engaged in chatting, talking, and laughing with the more comely ladies that he scarcely had time to introduce his poor wife, who sat like a wall-flower in the background, plainly dressed, and very conscious that her years of hard work and pinching and saving had robbed her of the very attractiveness which first charmed her husband. Only twice during the entire reception did I see this man introduce anyone to his wife, and then in a very perfunctory manner.

It could hardly seem possible that this very unattractive and apparently hard-working woman, in whom the joy of life was crushed out, could be the wife of this handsome, magnetic man, who, by the way, never liked to work, and who had not proposed to wear himself out, or worry himself to death, in getting a living.

I happened to know the history of this man's wealth, and that his success was due mostly to his wife's shrewdness—and as much to *her* hard work and self-denial as to his ability. Now that he has money and can afford to spend generously, he is in much demand and travels around the country —but his now unattractive wife is left at home, except on rare occasions.

As a young wife, she was too unselfishly devoted in her efforts to save and to help her husband get on in the world to spare her strength or have much time to preserve her beauty. She was willing to give her all to help; he let her do the worrying and the scrimping; and now he does not appreciate it. A very unattractive old age stares her in the face, while, though no older in years, he is in the flower of his manhood.

So much discord could be avoided in the home and so much joy introduced into it by a definite understanding and equal arrangement about household finances.

And when freedom and joy are each partner's share, they become the children's heritage. And a happy childhood is an imperative preparation for a happy maturity.

Most homes are far too serious. There are indeed many serious, too serious-minded fathers and mothers who do not wish to advertise their children to all the neighbors as "the laughing family." If this be so, yet, at the very least, these solemn parents may read the Bible. Where it is said, "Provoke not your children to wrath," it means literally, "Do not irritate your children"; "Do not rub them up the wrong way."

Children ought never to get the impression that they live in a hopeless, cheerless, cold world; but the household cheerfulness should transform their lives like sunlight, making their hearts glad with little things, rejoicing upon small occasion.

"How beautiful would our home-life be if every little child at the bedtime hour could look into the faces of the older ones and say: 'We've had such sweet times today.'"

"To love, and to be loved," says Sydney Smith, "is the greatest happiness of existence."

Your children are naturally as full of play as young kittens. They do not know anything about your business troubles. When they see you come home they ought to think of you as a new playfellow, fresh from the mysterious "down-town." They cannot imagine anything more important than to have fun—and you ought not have them think otherwise. You should want to keep the serious side of life from them as long as possible, to prolong their childhood, so that they may develop normally and their hearts may be tender and responsive to the noble things of life.

How many parents crush all the spontaneous, bubbling spirit out of the lives of their children by trying to make them adults in their childhood! It is a sorry day when a child gets the impression that his mother or father is not a playmate, or when the child does not long for the parents to come home so that they can have a good time.

Children become discouraged and disheartened when they are constantly told, "Don't do that," or "Get away." Their spontaneity is soon dampened and their enthusiasm quenched. Is there a more pitiable picture than long, anxious face upon a child, or lines of trouble already engraved upon youthful brows, and pallor where roses ought to be? What should the expression of maturity and care have to do with childish features? What have worry and anxiety about the future to do with childhood? Mothers and fathers, you do not know what you are doing when you rob your own flesh and blood of its childish joy. It is cruelty.

If optimism were woven into the very life and fiber of a child until it reached maturity, pessimism would have very little chance with it afterwards. The ideal father and mother will not allow fear, anxiety, or worry to stamp their hideous images upon a child's life. They will ensure that sunshine, sweetness, beauty, cheerfulness, and love will dominate the home so completely that there will be no chance for shadows, discord, and a thousand other enemies of happiness to do their deadly work.

Why not let the children dance and play to their heart's content? They will get rubs enough, knocks enough in the world; they will get enough of the hard side of life later. Resolve that they shall at least be *just as happy as you can make them* while at home, so that if they should have unfortunate experiences later, they can look back upon their home as a sweet, beautiful, charming oasis in their life; the happiest spot on earth.

It is a great thing to encourage fun in the home. There is nothing like a fun-loving home. It keeps children off the streets, it discourages vice and all that is morbid.

The home ought to be a sort of the theater for fun and all sorts of sports —a place where the children should take the active parts, although the parents should come in for a share, too. You will find that a little fun in the evening, romping, and playing with the children, will make you sleep better. It will clear the physical cobwebs and brain-ash from your mind. You will be fresher and brighter for it the next day. You will be surprised to see how much more work you can do, and how much more readily you can do it if you try to have all the innocent fun you can.

We have all felt the wonderful balm, the great uplift, the refreshment, the rejuvenation which have come from a good time with family. When we come home after a hard, exacting day's work, wherein our bodies were jaded and we were brain weary and exhausted, what magic a single hour's fun with family will often work in a tired soul!

Have fine music in the home.

Music tends to restore and preserve the mental harmony. Nervous diseases are wonderfully helped by good music. It keeps one's mind off one's troubles, and gives nature a chance to heal all sorts of mental discords.

"Music gives a soul to the universe, wings to the mind, flight to the imagination, a charm to sadness, gaiety and life to everything. It is the essence of order, and leads to all that is good, just, and beautiful," says Plato.

Happiness should begin in the home.

Half the misery in the world would be avoided if people would make a business of having *plenty of fun* at home, instead of running everywhere else in search of it.

There is an irrepressible longing for amusement, for rollicking fun, in young people, and if these longings were more fully met in the home it would not be so difficult to keep the boy and girl under the parental roof. I always think there is something wrong when the father or mother or the children are so very uneasy to get out of the house at night and to go off "somewhere" where they will have a good time. A happy, joyous home is a powerful magnet to all within it.

Swallow a lot of fun with your meals. The practice is splendid. It is he best thing in the world for your health. It is better than swallowing dyspepsia with every mouthful of food. Make cheerfulness the aim of the family gathering around the table. The meal time ought to be looked forward to by every member of the family as an occasion for a good time, for hearty laughter, and for bright, entertaining conversation. The children should be trained to bring their best moods and say their brightest and best things at the table. If this practice were put in force *it would revolutionize American homes and drive the doctors to despair.*

"Home" is the sweetest word in the language. It has ever been the favorite theme of the poet, the author, and the artist.

"What is more agreeable than one's home?" asked Cicero.

"Where we love is home," wrote Oliver Wendell Holmes. "Home that our feet may leave, but not our hearts."

It is the dream of "a home of my own" that lifts us all. There is no spur on earth which has had anything like the influence over the maturing boy or girl that his this vision of home. The thought of a filled with a loving spouse and children—dearer to one than life—keeps vast multitudes of men and women grinding away at their dreary tasks, when they see no other light in the distance.

To multitudes of people home is the only oasis in their desert life.

> *"'Mid pleasures and palaces thought we may roam,*
> *Be it ever so humble, there's no place like home."*

The home is the greatest power for good in the world. It ought to be, to paraphrase a Latin saying, the safest refuge to everyone.

To achieve this these worthy goals, make the following the mottoes hung over the entrance of your home, the words on your welcome mat: "Now for Rest and Happiness"; "No Discord Allowed Here."

Today I will...

- *Ask myself if I have taken the time to keep acquainted my family. Perhaps you have seen less of your sons and daughters in the years when they have been coming into manhood and womanhood than have their friends. You may know less of them than your neighbors do. If so, resolve to set time aside every day to befriend your spouse, your children—to show the same care and interest and attention to their activities and concerns as you do your work and your colleagues at work.*

- *Form the habit of locking all worries and concerns in the office or store at night, and resolve that whether business is a success or failure, my home shall be a success—the happiest, sweetest place on earth for me and mine. This will be a greater investment than any you will ever make in business.*

➡ *Remember that time moves on, that days pass by, and if I don't pay attention, my home will become just a house. Today is the moment I must tell my spouse I love him or her; tell my children I love them; play with my children; talk with my children and listen to their lives; talk with my spouse and listen to his or her life—not just what goes on at work, but the dreams, the goals, the worries, the concerns. Time moves on and the days pass by, and a family can slip away just as much as the hours.*

➡ _____
  _____

➡ _____
  _____

➡ _____
  _____

➡ _____
  _____

chapter 21

NATURE

Nature never wears a mean appearance.
Neither does the wisest man extort her secret and
lose his curiosity by finding out all her perfection.
—Emerson

The very presence of Nature is to many a great joy.

"Here is a bad, disagreeable day, as we call it," said Dr. Savage. "Shall we become unhappy because we get sprinkled and the black of our boots is spotted, or shall we learn to think of the wonder of the great forces that throughout the universe are playing round our little planet, sometimes, bursting through in sunshine, again draping the heavens in clouds, sometimes lifting up the waters and the dew from the ponds and the rivers and the lakes and the grass, again dropping them down in rain or sleet or snow, and so keeping the great forces of life and the changes of the world going their marvelous rounds? There is beauty in the leaden sky; there is God's wonder in every drop of rain; there are marvels that are infinite in a flake of snow. Shall we forget all this, and merely be troubled because they happen to come at a time when we who, in, our egotism, would desire to manage the universe, would have had the weather a little different?"

If we love beauty and look for it, we will see it wherever we go. If there is music in our souls, we will hear it everywhere; every object in nature will sing to us.

"If brain-weary over books and study," said Gladstone, "go out into the blessed sunlight and the pure air, and give heartfelt exercise to the body. The brain will soon become calm and rested."

How true it is that if we are cheerful and contented, all Nature appears to smile with us—the air seems more balmy, the sky more clear, the earth has a brighter green, the trees have a richer foliage, the flowers are more fragrant, the birds sing more sweetly, and the sun, moon, and stars all appear more beautiful.

"Twelve years ago," said Walt Whitman once, "I came to Camden to die. But everyday I went into the country, bathed in the sunshine, lived with the birds and squirrels, and played in the water with the fishes. I received my health from Nature."

"It is the unqualified result of all my experience with the sick," said Florence Nightingale, "that second only to their need of fresh air is their need of light; that, after a close room what most hurts them is a dark room; and that it is not only light, but direct sunshine they want."

"Sunlight," says Dr. L. W. Curtis in *Health Culture*, "has much to do in keeping air in a healthy condition. No plant can grow in the dark, neither can man remain healthy in a dark, ill-ventilated room. When the first asylum for the blind was erected in Massachusetts, the committee decided to save expense by not having any windows. They reasoned that, as the patients could not see, there was no need of any light. It was built without windows, but ventilation was well provided for, and the poor sightless patients were domiciled in the house. But things did not go well: one after another began to sicken, and great languor fell upon them; they felt distressed and restless, craving something, they hardly knew what. After two had died and all were ill, the committee decided to have windows. The sunlight poured in, and the white faces recovered their color; their flagging energies and depressed spirits revived, and health was restored."

The sun, making all living things to grow, exerts its happiest influence to cheering our minds and making our hearts glad. If we have sunshine in our souls, we will go on our ways rejoicing, content to look forward if under a cloud, not bating one jot of heart or hope if for a moment cast down; not only happy ourselves, but giving happiness to others.

Water, air, and sunshine, the three greatest hygienic agents, are free, and within the reach of all. And yet, how many of us walk across a park, or a common, or a public garden early in the morning on our way to work, and though here is a setting all radiant with beauty, bidding for attention, we walk by unconscious of it all—looking ahead to the world of work and missing the world of beauty that might well have made all the difference in how we arrived at work and performed our work?

How many of us drive from one appointment or meeting to the next with that same careless indifference—while all the while, bird and brook and wild flower are vying with one another to arouse us from some absorption in business problems; masses of liveliness smile from flower beds, from blossom, shrub, and tree without attracting even a passing glance?

Let us not become so absorbed in making a living that we have no time to make a life.

Let us not become so taken up with putting money in our purses that we have no time to put beauty into our lives.

Let us, instead, be like Ruskin and others, for whom every natural object, every flower, every plant, every tree, every sunset, awakened delights that would ravish an angel.

Today I will…

- *Go to a park, a stream, the ocean, and let myself commune with nature. There is no better listener than nature; she not only listens patiently, but in beauty. Take the problems that are hemming you in within the four walls of your office or home, and bring them to nature to listen to. You will find an expansiveness in your thought, a spaciousness between your worries where serenity can enter.*

- *Hug a tree. This may sound like environmentalist talk, and perhaps you find that off-putting. For a moment, however, disabuse yourself of that perception. You can embrace nature without having to embrace the beliefs of naturalists, environmentalists, etc. Go to a park, the woods, or even to a tree in your back yard, and press your arms around it, your body up against it. You will feel something alive. It will be the tree, and it will be you.*

→ *Go on a nature hike. Park services, local nature clubs, and the like organize nature hikes in many cities. Sign up for one. You will be amazed and affected by the discovery that the world of nature is as alive and intricate as is yours, struggles for the same livelihood as you do, and has been working at making its home on the same part of the earth as have you—and in many instances, has been working at making its home there long before you arrived.*

→ _____
_____

→ _____
_____

→ _____
_____

→ _____
_____

chapter 22

THE JOYS OF IMAGINATION

*The soul without imagination is what
an observatory would be without a telescope.*
—Henry Ward Beecher

I know of an elderly, Italian lady who has, for many years, been an invalid and has rarely been out of her house, and yet she says she has the most delightful times imaginable on her mental vacations. She travels abroad every day, revisits the scenes familiar in her childhood, climbs the Alps, and walks through the streets of the cities of Italy, once so dear to her. She rides the wind as she sits for hours on the veranda of her old Sorrento home, watching sailboats skimming across the bay of Naples. She watches the oranges and lemons ripening on the trees. She takes mental trips to the leading theaters, and reviews again the plays and operas which she saw in her younger days. She reads Shakespeare, and sees all the great Shakespearean actors and actresses in her mind's eye, who never tire of repeating their roles for her. Oftentimes when in pain she takes off on her mental trips, and when she comes back she is refreshed with new hope and new courage for fighting her physical battles. For hours, this sweet lady not only forgets all aches and pains which make her an invalid, she forgets the physical chains which enslave her in doors—and she wanders over the earth at will. These mental trips, she says, are often more enjoyable than the physical ones, because she has none of the annoyances and discomforts of travel and none of the expense. She says that if people only knew the possibilities of enjoyment through the picturing power of the imagination, the whole human race would be happy.

Regrettably, our training and education do not half emphasize the possibilities of enjoyment through the imagination, which is ever available to each of us, to transport us in the twinkling of an eye into whatever we can dream.

One of the great secrets of those who surprise everybody by the enormous amount of work they accomplish and pleasure they experience in the midst of what for others would be stress, is their ability to take frequent mental recesses. Little vacations. I know, for example, several people so hemmed in and confined by perpetual hard work that it is almost impossible for them to be long away from their places of business or their professions —yet although they are subject to conditions that would worry others into an early grave, they always seem to be serene, fresh, and buoyant, because they have acquired the happy art of taking mental vacations. I have interviewed some of these people, and they tell me that no matter how trying, or how exasperating their work, or how annoying the conditions may be about them, they seek opportunities to lift themselves out of their troubles and into a harmonious and blissful mental condition which nothing material can touch or mar. They have so educated their imaginations that they can create new worlds and live in them. They go back to the old home or farm and relive happy moments from their childhood days and friendships. They wade and fish in brooks, climb mountains, tramp in the forest, and meander through the meadows.

It does not take long to freshen a jaded mind if one knows the secret art. And that is the art of imagination. The imaginative faculties are wings which enable us to soar away quickly into joys ineffable—to fly away at will from our harassing, embarrassing, unwanted, surroundings; from things that discourage, disgust, and annoy; from lives of grasping and deadlines and drudgery; from the "blues."

Imagination helps the prisoner to fly out of the cell. John Bunyan was in prison when he wrote his masterpiece *The Pilgrim's Progress*. He used his imaginative faculty to create such characters as Christian, Evangelist, Faithful, Hopeful, and Giant Despair—fictitious characters who representative of moods, feelings, beliefs, attitudes, and capacities of human nature, live forever in our hearts.

No matter how badly things may be about us or what blunders or mistakes harass us, no matter what misfortunes overtake us, imagination is to our opportunity for happiness in times of duress like the captured bird which the young boys harass, tease, and torment, but which wrenches away from them and in an instant soars into the ether and is free again.

Whoever has a good imagination, well-developed, ought never to have a dull moment. Those with trained imaginations are largely independent of their environments. If things are disagreeable, if people bore them, if their surroundings are uncongenial, they can lift themselves out of it all and retire within the gates of their imaginations, and revel in the exercise of their imaginative faculties. In an instant, they can be in an ideal world of the imagination, where the sources of happiness are inexhaustible.

The great truth of happiness, is that the sacred longings of the imagination are give us as constant reminders that we can make our lives sublime; that no matter how disagreeable or unfriendly our surroundings my be, we can lift ourselves into the ideal conditions that we see in our imaginative vision.

Today I will...

- → *Have fun playing the world of my imagination. The imagination is an incredible resource of diversion, creativity, problem-solving, goal-setting, etc. Spend some time today creating imaginary scenarios for world peace, interplanetary travel, outlandish solutions or alternatives to your current concerns and circumstances, etc. If you make your imaginings vivid, you will return from this respite from your day feeling uplifted and enthusiastic—better able to apply yourself to the realities that are before you, and possibly even having acquired insights into your current endeavors and circumstances.*

- → *Remind myself that it has been said that what the mind can conceive, the mind can achieve. Spending time in imagining is not all frivolous. Your imagination can be the source of what tomorrow will become your life. Imagine the circumstances you would like to be in tomorrow (not necessarily the day after today, but some foreseeable future time). If you continue to vividly entertain this vision daily, you will find that your actions and thoughts may well begin moving you in the direction you are envisioning.*

→ *Apply not only my intellect to some situation, but also my imagination. Your imagination allows you to "play outside of the box," to discover new possibilities. Einstein said "Imagination is greater than knowledge." Don't just follow what you've done in the past, what you know—open up your imagination and see where it leads you. For example, rather than just making your bed tonight, change the arrangement of furniture in your bedroom—or some other room in your home. Or change the arrangement of furniture in your office. By imagining new possibilities in these everyday circumstances, you will be exercising your imagination for discoveries in a myriad of circumstances.*

→ _____
_____

→ _____
_____

→ _____
_____

→ _____
_____

chapter 23

THE STRAIN TO KEEP UP APPEARANCES KILLS HAPPINESS

*Fine words and insinuating appearances
are seldom associated with true virtue.*
—*Confucius*

The struggle to keep up with those in better circumstances is one of the tragedies of the times. Not long ago, for instance, the home of a New York widow and all her other property that the law did not exempt, were sold at auction. It was found that this over-ambitious mother, in her efforts to marry her daughters into families much above their station, had made desperate efforts to keep up appearances, and had run into debts which had finally cost her her home. The family, it turned out, could have lived in comfort on her modest income, but for the mother's misguided values. Instead, it was found that she owed large amounts to the florists, the caterers, the milliners, and the dry goods people, and that she had been living for a long time far beyond her income, keeping up appearances which were perpetual lies. Thousands of dollars were, squandered in buying hats, dresses, expensive laces, and all sorts of finery, so that her daughters might shine as brilliantly as other young women who had many times their means. All this she did because of her ambition to marry her daughters to rich men. Now the mother is without a home and the daughters remain still without husbands.

This striving to keep up appearances causes much of the unhappiness in homes. Why is it that people burn out their lives with discontent and misery, making slaves of themselves to keep up appearances, when they might be so contented and happy, might be somebody and stand for something were they not so money-mad, and ambition-crazy?

It is not so much our lack of comforts or of luxury, as our envy, our mistaken values that make us unhappy.

What terrible inconvenience, hardship, and suffering we endure on account of how e want to appear in other people's eyes and opinions! What foolish slaves we make of ourselves because of what other people think! How we scheme and contrive to make them think we are other than we really are!

It is our excessive regard for the approval in other people's eyes that make us unhappy and discontented with our lot, that make us strain and struggle and slave, in order to keep up false appearances.

I know families in New York who live in perpetual misery because of this condition of things. I have in mind a business man who has a very small income, but both he and his wife are educated, cultured, and have refined tastes, and they simply will not live in a part of the city in keeping with their income. They insist on living in one of the more fashionable neighborhoods, with the result being that they are obliged to strain so much to do so, that they have very little for food and clothing and recreation after paying rent.

Many people seem to think that it disgrace not to have a big income; that the great desideratum of life is to be able to spend a lot of money upon luxuries. But, after all is said and done, what is there in it? Often, only unhappiness.

Undoubtedly, ambition stands in the way of more people's contentment and happiness than almost anything else. The foolish determination to do what others do, to get ahead of others and to be able to live as they do, to have the luxuries and comforts of people who are better off than they—this over-vaulting ambition is one of the great happiness enemies.

It is a false ambition which keeps us pulling and hauling and straining to do something which somebody else has done, not because we need it ourselves, not because it would add a particle to our comfort or real welfare or because it is really worthwhile, but because we are eaten up with the consuming ambition for the desire to outshine others, to outdo them, to get ahead of them, to live a little better off than they, to have a little better home, a little better house in a little better part of the town, to dress our children a little better, to surround ourselves with more luxuries.

But are these things really helpful, are they really worth while?

No.

Growth, enlargement of life, enrichment of one's nature—these are the things that are worthwhile.

Ambition to stand for more in the community, to push our horizon of ignorance farther and farther away from us, to think a little higher each day, to think a little more of ourselves, to have a little more faith in ourselves and in everybody else—this is the ambition of real use in the world, which, if achieved, brings contentment and true happiness.

I know a man who has made quite a distinguished success in his specialty and yet he is as uneasy, dissatisfied, and discontented as any man I know. He is always comparing himself with people who have been more successful, who have done more and better work in his line and who have accumulated more money. The sight of people who have gotten along faster, the thought of their living better, or having a better reputation, more fame, irritates him. His eyes are so intent upon others' accomplishments and what they have that he seems blind to what he has accomplished and what he has. His own surroundings mean scarcely anything to him.

He has an ideal family, a noble wife, superb children, and although his home is not as sumptuous or commodious, nor his environment as luxurious or grand as that of some of his neighbors, yet he has a multitude of advantages over them. Somehow, his strong constitution, his healthy and harmonious family do not seem to count for very much with him.

He has a far-away look in his eyes; his gaze is so set upon what others do and what others have, that he does not seem to know how to appreciate his own, and he is always castigating himself for not working harder, and getting on more rapidly, notwithstanding the fact that he is always overworking and never takes time to cultivate friendships or to enjoy social life.

If every day he would stop for a few minutes and empty his mind of his envy and jealousy, would thrust out his false ambition and try to appreciate his own instead of forever thinking of what others have, if every morning he would congratulate himself upon his good fortune in having such a happy and harmonious family—a beautiful wife and fine robust children—

when many of those whom he envies have to bear all sorts of marital discords and troubles, he would learn to appreciate his own blessings. In thinking how fortunate he is in his happy environment, he would develop a capacity for appreciation, and what others have would lose its peculiar fascination.

Many of us miss the joys that might be ours by keeping our eyes fixed on those of other people. None of us can enjoy our own opportunities for happiness while we are envious of another's. We lose a great deal of the joy of living by not cheerfully accepting the small pleasures that come to us every day, instead of longing and wishing for what belongs to others. We do not take any pleasure in our own modest car, because we long for the luxurious limousine that some one else owns. The edge is taken off the enjoyment of our own little home because we are watching the palatial residence of our neighbor. Life has its full measure of happiness for every one of us if we would only make up our minds to make the very most of every opportunity that comes our way, instead of longing for the things that come our neighbor's way.

All the wonderful details of little experiences, the fine courtesies, the exquisite things of life, the things that are worthwhile, are so often lost to us because we live at such a terrific pace to catch up to others. We cannot take time to see things, to appreciate them, to enjoy them. We do not take time to enjoy our friends. Our whole mind is too often and too much anxiously focused upon the person's life in front of us.

The sort of ambition which must be always condemned is that in which vanity figures most conspicuously, and in which the praise and admiration of the world are the object sought—rather than to be of use in the world, to be a leader in the service of humanity, and to be the noblest, best, and most efficient that one can be.

The world is full of happiness, and there is always plenty to go round, if we are only willing to take the kind that comes our way. Instead, though, how many of us are like the buttercup that grew in the field beside the daisy. The buttercup was discontented and envied the daisy "for daisies grow so trim and tall," and she always had a longing to wear a frill around her neck too. But a robin, who was flying by, heard her lamentation and told her how foolish she was to want to be a made-up daisy instead of her own bright self. He told her to

> *"Look bravely up into the sky*
> *And be content with knowing*
> *That God wished for a buttercup*
> *Just here where you are growing."*

The way we accept life and the interpretation we give to our experiences is the determining factor in our enjoyment or disappointment in this world.

Today I will…

- *Appreciate what I have and not envy what others have. In our world, it is easy to become envious of what others have. Everything is tugging at us to "keep up with the Joneses." But in envying others, we are diminishing ourselves—making ourselves too small for happiness.*

- *Remember that "the grass always looks greener on the other side." We look at those around us, at their possessions, and we think that their possessions are reflections of their happiness. But that's a delusion. Everyone has problems, and if we possessed everything that others had that we wanted, we would be no less without problems. Better to be content with what we have and know the enjoyment of it, experience the happiness of it, than to delude ourselves into thinking that if we only had more, we would finally and forever be happy. Those who own a better car than we may be happier than we, but it is not because of the make, year, or model of their car.*

- *Remind myself that to place my happiness in striving after appearances is to place my source of happiness outside of my self. To strive to keep up with appearances is to remove the power for happiness from yourself and place it in things. But if things outside of you possess the power to bring you happiness, and if every year something new is brought out into the marketplace, then unless you can afford to replace what you have every year and purchase what is new, then your source of happiness will always be ahead of your ability to be happy.*

→ _____
  _____
→ _____
  _____
→ _____
  _____
→ _____
  _____

chapter 24

THE TRAGEDY OF POSTPONED ENJOYMENT

"The mill will never grind with the water that has passed"

Many of us, instead of finding our happiness in things close at hand and in our everyday associations and experiences, look to the future and long for other days and other conditions—when we assure ourselves that we shall obtain perfect happiness. It is but a vain dream! The hour never comes and never will. "He who does not find content and satisfaction today, who does not rejoice in the sunshine and the blessings God gives him moment by moment, will never find the path to Paradise and will live and die discontented."

There was once a very brilliant and charming young man who made up his mind that he was going to devote the first half of his life to amassing a million dollars—and the balance of his life in the unstinted enjoyment of his money. He resolved to sacrifice every conflicting desire in pursuit of his one unwavering aim—to cut off everything which could possibly conflict with his life purpose. He hushed the great longing in his heart for music and sacrificed his soul's calling for the beautiful, for art. Later, he felt sure, he would revel in art and music.

But when he had made his first million he found that his ambition called for another million, so he resolved to work a little longer and then quit when he had two million. When he reached that point, however, his ambition had grown to monstrous proportions and kept calling for more, more. He resolved nevertheless to break away and to enjoy what he had. But he soon found that he was slaving under ambition's lash—and he kept going on and on, making greater sacrifices of his finer nature, until one day he caught a glimpse of himself in a long mirror. For a moment he could not believe his eyes. But the truth very soon became painfully evident, and he resolved then and there to quit the money game and to start on his quest of pleasure.

But he found that he had lost his taste for many of the things which had called to him so loudly in his youthful blood. When he began to travel, he found that the great masterpieces of architecture, painting, and sculpture—which he had dreamed would give him such pleasure—were like closed books to his mind, because his aesthetic faculties had become so atrophied that they no longer responded to stimulus.

Returning home, he then resolved that he would make it his business to surround himself with friends for the balance of his life. But he soon discovered that friendship faculties, too, had gone out of service for lack of exercise. He had learned the skill of making a dollar but not the skill of making friends.

He felt sure that music, his first love, had not gone back on him, and he went to the great centers of music to revel in the opera. But he soon found that his ability to appreciate lacking.

And so, in his desperation, he turned from one thing to another, trying to enjoy himself. Even dissipation no longer could give him satisfaction. He had lost all power of enjoyment; his fortune but a mockery to him. He had sacrificed youth, health, friends, days, music, art, and literature. He had become a burned-out old man with a fortune, but with no power to enjoy it. He had money, but nothing else.

"The pitiful part of this inalienable right to the pursuit of happiness," says Charles Dudley Warner, "is that most people interpret it to mean the pursuit of wealth, and strive for that always, postponing being happy until they get a fortune. And if they are lucky in that, find in the end that happiness has somehow eluded them; that, in short, they have not cultivated that in themselves which alone can bring happiness."

One of the greatest tragedies of life is the postponement of enjoyment. The great regret of most people when nearing the end of life is that they did not live as they went along, that they attempted to postpone their enjoyment instead of living to the full each day as it came.

To postpone enjoyment day after day and year after year until we get more money or a better position is to cheat ourselves not only of present enjoyment, but also of the power to enjoy in the future. The only way to be happy is to take advantage of, to nurture, the little opportunities that come to us to brighten life as we go along.

And yet, how often do we see young people start out in life with small capital and work like slaves for years, putting aside every opportunity for pleasure or relaxation, denying themselves the luxury of an occasional outing, attendance at a theater or concert, a trip to the country or the purchase of a coveted book—even postponing their reading and general culture until they have more leisure, more money! They delude themselves with the thought that when the following year arrives they will take life easier, perhaps indulge in some of these desired things, but when next year comes they think they must economize a little longer. Thus they put off every enjoyment from year to year. Then, at length a time comes when they decide they can afford to indulge in a little pleasure. They go abroad, or try to enjoy music or works of art, or attempt to broaden their minds by reading and studying. But it is too late. They have become hopelessly wedged into the rut the years have made about them. The freshness of life has departed. Enthusiasm has fled. The fires of ambition have died down. The long years of waiting have crushed the capacity to enjoy. And the possessions for which they sacrificed all their natural and healthy longings for joy and brightness have turned to Dead Sea fruit.

Many people have lost their lives while chasing after a hat, an umbrella, a package, or a child's ball that rolls in front of an oncoming car. "What a sad and terrible loss of life," we say. And rightly so. But how many have lost their lives chasing after a few more dollars—and not until it's too late, if even then, do we see the sad and terrible loss of life *there*.

The sacrifices we make, the price we pay for our fortunes, is something appalling. Does it pay to sacrifice the very things for which we're alive to get together a little more money? A *lot* more money? Do those who gloat over the fact that they are getting ahead much faster than others around them ever notice what they are losing on their way to wealth, their race to riches?

How many of us notice that while we are "gaining," we are often losing something which is infinitely more precious?

Nature keeps a one-priced store. She lets you take whatever you want, but you pay the price for it, and you often leave that which is infinitely more valuable than what you take. How many take the hours from each day and leave their characters in exchange! How many swap their ability, their education, their passion for dollars! How many exchange all that is finest, most delicate, and sweetest in their natures!

Those who cultivate the habit of enjoyment, who avail themselves of the opportunity to indulge in innocent pleasures, to brighten and broaden their lives by listening to good music or looking at works of art, by studying the beauties of nature or reading an inspiring book, will unconsciously find themselves far ahead in the race for success.

Too many of us do not count our blessings or truly open our hearts to enjoy them, till the golden hour has gone by forever—and we look back too late on all that we might have had and made and done. How many make slaves of themselves, pinching, scrimping, and practicing a grinding economy all through the best years of their lives, with the firm belief that they are getting ready for great enjoyment in the future!

There is nothing more delusive than the idea that we are going to do something tomorrow which we believe we cannot afford the time to do today.

Oh, the waste of life, the precious years lost in getting ready to enjoy! Oh, the delusion of always putting the time of enjoyment in the future, forever deferring good things until the tissues have hardened and the nerves have lost their power to carry agreeable sensations! How many people there are who murder their capacity for enjoyment and make slaves of themselves in trying to hoard up that which they might have enjoyed in their younger days, and which will be but a mockery to them late in life!

It seems strange that level-headed business men and women who have been such a success in their fields should not be able to see that they cannot really enjoy themselves after retiring from an active, busy life unless they have all along been developing a broad range of interests outside of their specialties. If we have not been attending musical performances during our working years, developing our love and ear for music, the chances are that we will be bored to death through a performance if it is only upon retirement that we finally try to exercise this interest. How could we expect to enjoy an opera if throughout our lives our musical tastes and faculties have not been being developed?

And what about art? Let the average business person visit the great art galleries after years of laboring at a desk and having his or her interests occupied with such matters as profits, losses, deadlines, and competition, and the odds are that he or she will get tired of walking through an art museum inside of two days—his or her mind having not been trained in such appreciation. A lifetime of singular activity in a business career would not have developed qualities which would help in the appreciation of the beauties of art, or to measure the spiritual value of art to life, or to see the meaning in the great masterpieces.

Or let the high-level executive try travel upon retirement. Many are unable to enjoy it without filling it with activities, so used are they to lives of busyness. They return from what is intended to be a time of leisure and boast, instead, about the many places they saw, things they did—in a word, their accomplishments. It has all become just another means of conducting business, of arranging and scheduling activities. How few can simply sit on a beach or attend a concert—not to gloat over what great seats their money bought, but simply to give opportunity to their finer sensibilities?

Even on vacations, how many of us find our minds frequently reverting to and wondering about the colleagues or business projects for which reason we took our vacations to leave behind! After a few days on vacation, how many find that the faculties which have been made dominant by so many years of active service keep pulling them towards thoughts of the affairs of their business or profession, the people and associations at work?

The great secret of happiness is to learn to enjoy as we go along. Every day should be a holiday in the highest sense of the word. It is out of the ordinary activities, the common, routine affairs of the ordinary day—in the home, in the store, in the factory—dealing with common, homely, everyday circumstances, that we ultimately manufacture life and all that it means to us.

No matter how busy we are, something should be brought into every day's experience which will enlarge, broaden, and enrich our minds. Every day should add a new layer of beauty and joy to *the sum total* of our life before today gives way to tomorrow. It was not intended that one part of life should be filled with joy and the remainder be left barren.

It doesn't pay to look forward to enjoyment. A writer once said, "I would as soon chase butterflies for a living or bottle moonshine for a cloudy night. The only way to be happy is to take the drops of happiness given us every day of our lives. The student must learn to be happy while plodding over his or her lessons, the apprentice while he is learning his or her trade, the merchant while making his or her fortune, or they will be sure to miss their enjoyment when they have gained what they have signed for."

There is an Eastern legend of a powerful genius, who promised a beautiful maiden a gift of rare value if she would pass through a field of corn, and, without pausing, without going backwards or wandering hither and thither, select the largest and ripest ear—the value of the gift to be in proportion to the size and perfection of the ear she should choose. She passed through the field, seeing a great many ears well worth gathering, but was always hoping to find a larger and more perfect one. She passed them all by until eventually she came to a part of the field where the stalks grew more stunted. These, she knew, would not win her her prize, and so she passed by them, too—until she eventually discovered that she had passed through the entire field without having selected anything.

This little fable is a faithful picture of many of our lives, in which we are rejecting the good things that are on our way and within our reach for something which we presume will lie ahead as our reward—something for which we vainly hope, but find we seldom ever secure.

How few of us realize until too late that on a dark night and in a dangerous place, where the footing is insecure, a simple lantern in the hand is worth a dozen stars.

How many of us will go through life with our eyes fixed on a distant goal, straining every nerve to reach it? And on our way, we will pass indescribable beauties of earth and sky, and innumerable opportunities to help others over rough places—occasions to brighten and beautify the commonplace life of every day—but we will see them not. Or seeing them, we will not pause to give time to them, but will beg our apologies, claiming that there is just so much that we have to do that we cannot stop.

Heedless of all that does not point directly toward what we consider the winning post, we forge onward toward our envisioned destination to find—what? That we have, perhaps, gained the wealth we sought, the secrets of fame, satisfied our ambition—but at the cost of all that sweetens, beautifies, ennobles, and enriches life. Having gained the fine house that we sought, we find that we have become so bound by our business, so absorbed in the everyday routines and long hours, that enjoyment of it as a *home* must ever be pushed further ahead until we can spare a little more time from our work.

We are always looking ahead, past this moment and *its* opportunities to provide us with those joys that we only see in our future circumstances. There seems some strange propensity in human nature to locate all the good things of life in an existence that is yet to come.

If we would only realize that the things that we are striving to acquire in the future are ever and always about us now, we would grow by leaps and bounds.

Happiness is something that we must take as we go along, or we lose it. When the Children of Israel were passing through the desert they were fed with manna fresh every day. Some of the people did not have faith enough to trust the Lord to feed them every day, so they tried to store up some of this manna for future use. But it spoiled. They soon learned that they could not keep manna for the future. Moreover, in attempting to do so, they were denying themselves of the manna of today.

Our happiness is like this manna. We must gather it anew every day we live.

Everywhere we see people who are trying to store up as manna for the future what was intended for their daily happiness. They, too, too often find to their surprise that what they have been postponing enjoying has spoiled, evaporated, would not keep—that it must be used as we go along; that we must use happiness when fresh, like fresh plucked flowers.

There are a great many things—good impulses—which are good for today, but not for tomorrow. How many people delay kindness, the expression of love, until the person is dead or beyond their reach, and then try to atone for a neglected past by flowers and tears at the funeral!

Today is the day to say the kind word that springs to your lips, to obey the generous impulse that stirs your heart. These people who haunt your mind, and whom you promise yourself that you will help "someday," need your help now, and you can give it more readily now than at any other time. Because now is the only time you truly have.

Every tomorrow has, in addition to its own cares and duties, all those which were neglected in the past, while its opportunities and possibilities are no greater than are those of today or were those of yesterday.

Don't defer your happiness until you get rich. You may be surprised to find that your manna has spoiled, that you should have eaten it when first given.

Deferred happiness and the deferred good deed do not keep.

How we deceive ourselves. We are always getting ready to live, neglecting the present, focusing our eyes upon the future, always straining for something yet to come, and never half appreciating what we have, or enjoying as we go along. Why do we allow the mirage of tomorrow to keep our eyes from the beauties of today? Why do we allow anticipated joys to blind us to those that are close by us? We trample down the violets and the daisies trying to reach the larger blossoms on the trees.

They alone are happy who have learned to extract happiness not from ideal conditions but from the actual ones about them. Those who have has mastered this secret will not wait for ideal surroundings; will not wait until next year, next decade—until they get rich, until they can travel abroad, until they can afford to surround themselves with works of the great masters, or whatever. They will make the most possible of what they have now.

Those who have spent all the best years of their lives neglecting everything outside of the rut and routine in which they are spending their lives will be lost when they get out of it. They will find that outside of the few tracks in their brains formed by their routine lives, they get very little satisfaction—because they have all along not been developing their *whole* brain, their whole beings.

"We treat our joys as one of my neighbors did her choice currants," says a writer. "'Let's have a pie,' said this woman's children when the bushes began to bear. But the mother would not hear of using such fine fruit while green; it must ripen. When the currants were ripe, the children begged them for the table, but the mother had decided to save them for jelly. When jelly-making was proposed, she wanted to wait until other work was out of the way, and she could 'do it as it ought to be done.' But lo, when she was fully ready, the sun, the birds, and an unexpected storm, had all been there before her, and the bushes were bare!

"That's the way we do with our blessings and gladnesses—the mercies that are 'new every morning.' We say, 'Oh, how I could enjoy this if'—and then we let the trial, foreboding, or trouble crowd it out of place. Some day we expect to be ready really to enjoy our health, our home, our friends; but who can promise us that when that long postponed day comes, the fruit will still be on the bushes?"

Today I will...

> Take time out to play more, laugh more, enjoy myself more. Experience the moments of and times for happiness that I deserve today. I will remember the proverb "All work and no play makes Jack [and Jill] a dull boy [girl]."

> Remind myself that the saying "Don't put off until tomorrow what you can do today" applies not only to work and tasks and chores and duties and obligations, but also to happiness, joy, and fun. As Goethe said, "Nothing is worth more than today."

> Remind myself that "saving for a rainy day" is a good policy, but it can also cause me to overlook the many enjoyable opportunities that are available to me in the sunshine of today.

> Remember how many times I've said, "Oh, I'd love to do that," only to find out that when I finally made the time to "do that," the "that" was gone. Today I'll do it!

> At the grocery store I'll purchase something that's not on my shopping list, something that's frivolous and just happens to catch my eye. A treat for me. Something new. Something I've never tried, but that intrigues me—that catches my eye, that looks like it would be fun to try.

> I'll do something silly, whimsical, playful, goofy—something completely "out of character."

> I'll tell a stranger something kind; I'll tell someone at work how attractive, how handsome, how kind—whatever it is I'm

feeling—he or she is; I'll speak what's in my heart that I ordinarily put off speaking because I've been afraid of being embarrassed or rejected.

→ *I will not wait for "that someone special" to enter my life in order to be happy. Give yourself a candlelight dinner at home; take a bubble bath; light incense in your bedroom; buy flowers for your table. Don't make other people or other times responsible for your happiness.*

→ _____
_____

→ _____
_____

→ _____
_____

chapter 25

THE TWIN ENEMIES OF HAPPINESS: FEAR AND WORRY

"There is no use talking," said a woman. "Every time I move,
I vow I'll never move again. Such neighbors as I get in with!
Seems as though they grow worse and worse."
"Indeed?" replied her caller. "Perhaps you take the
worst neighbor with you when you move."

Once upon a time, a magician felt such pity for a mouse in his house which lived in perpetual fear of the cat, that he changed it into a cat. But it at once began to be afraid of the dog, and the magician changed it into a dog It still suffered constant terror of a tiger on the premises, and the magician turned it into a tiger. Nor did its troubles end there, for it was in constant fear of a huntsman. Finally the disgusted magician turned it back to a mouse again, saying, "As you have only the nerve of a mouse, it is impossible to help you by giving you the body of a nobler animal."

There are no more enemies of happiness than fear and worry. They are always and everywhere a curse. There is nothing which we are called upon to meet in life, there is no misfortune or disaster that can ever come to us which we cannot bear better without these joy killers. We should fight against such influences which tend to depress the mind as we would against a temptation to crime.

Fear is an old, old enemy, indeed, and worry its hated accomplice. Primitive fear we have always had with us, but worry is the disease of our own age. In our "enlightenment," we both pity and ridicule primitive tribal people who lived—and of those remaining today, still do live—in mortal fear of their cruel gods. But have we not also created our equally exacting demons before which *our* souls cringe and *our* powers wither and fail?

Fear kills hope; worry and anxiety crush confidence, ruin the power to concentrate, and paralyze the initiative. Fear is the fatal foe of all achievement. It is the poisoner of happiness, the parent of worry. Moreover, it is not so much the great sorrows, the great burdens, the great hardships, the great calamities that cloud over the sunshine of life, as the little, petty vexations, insignificant anxieties and fear, the little daily dyings, which render our lives unhappy and destroy our mental elasticity without advancing our lives one inch.

"Anxiety never yet bridged any chasm."

How can people expect to become happy and contended who are always dwelling upon their miseries, misfortunes, and sorrows, always expressing discontent in their thoughts and actions? We should all remember that there is no philosophy in which it is taught that a negative mental attitude can produce its opposite!

Yet despite our knowing this, many never seem to be able to rid their minds of fear and worry. The are always afraid of, worried about something. When they are poor they imagine that if they only had money and health they would never feel dread or worry again. They imagine that if they had this or that, if they were differently environed or conditioned, they could get rid of anxiety and its whole vampire family, but when they gain these prizes, the same old enemy, although in a different form, still pursues them. In the end, they ultimately do not have courage enough to truly enjoy life. They are afraid to mingle with those who are mentally their superiors, or who have been more favored by fortune or looks—fearful that their poverty of mind or purse or appearance may be disclosed, or their presumed poverty of appearance would be evident. They thus forfeit many advantages and pleasures to be derived from social discourse. They have become cowardly—and cowards are never happy.

Among a multitude of people, a dread of some impending evil is ever present. It haunts them even in their happiest moments. They are never so well as their neighbors. The weather never suits them. The climate is trying. The winds are too high or too low; it is too hot or too cold, too damp or too dry. The roads are either muddy or dusty. Their minds are so affected by the chronic anxiety and fear that something is going to happen to them, are so troubled with foreboding thoughts, that their judgment is not reliable. Instead, fear steps in and good sense, good judgment, steps out. Their joy is poisoned by fear, so that they never take real pleasure or comfort in anything. The skeleton in the closet is the ghost that is ever at the banquet.

"I met Mr. N. one wet morning," says Dr. John Todd; "and, 'bound as I was to make the best of it, I ventured, 'Good morning. This rain will be fine for your grass crop.'

"'Yes, perhaps,' he replied, 'but it is very bad for corn; I don't think we'll have half a crop.'

"A few days later, I met him again. 'This is a fine sun for corn, Mr. N.'

"'Yes,' said he, 'but it's awful for rye; rye wants cold weather.'

"One cool morning soon after, I said: 'This is a capital day for rye.'

'Yes,' he said, 'but it is the worst kind of weather for corn and grass; they want heat to bring them forward.'"

There are a vast number of fidgety, nervous, and eccentric people who live only to expect new disappointments or to recount their old ones.

"Impatient people," said Spurgeon, "water their miseries, and hoe up their comforts."

"Let's see," said a neighbor to a farmer, whose wagon was loaded down with potatoes, "weren't we talking together last August?"

"I believe so."

"At that time, you said corn was all burnt up."

"Yes."

"And potatoes were baking in the ground."

"Yes."

"And that your district could not possibly expect more than half a crop."

"I remember."

"Well, here you are with your wagon loaded down. Things didn't turn out so badly, after all—eh?"

"Well, no-o," said the farmer, as he raked his fingers through his hair, "but I tell you my geese suffered awfully for want of a mud hole to paddle in."

What is a pessimist but "a man who looks on the sun only as a thing that casts a shadow"?

In a life of constant worrying, we are as much behind the times as if we were to go back to the steam engines that wasted 90% of the energy of the coal, instead of having an electric dynamo that utilized 90% of the power. We waste so much of our energy in fretting and stewing, in useless anxiety, in scolding, in complaining about the weather and the perversity of inanimate things.

Too many of us nurse our troubles as women nurse their babies. "Troubles grow larger," said Lady Holland, "by nursing."

To a great extent, much of our sense of fear comes about because our theologies and our creeds have too much anxiety and fear, too much shadow, and too little joys and gladness, too much cloud and too little of the sunshine, too much of the hereafter and too little of the now and here. It is "the Christ and not the creed" that humanity wants.

There is also among a vast multitude of us a fear of disease, which mars their happiness. They picture the horrible symptoms of some dread malady they are sure is developing in their systems. Their constant fear in fact actually impairs their bodies' nutrition and weakens their bodies' resisting power, tending to encourage or develop any possible hereditary taint or disease tendency which may indeed be lurking in their systems. Moreover, what depresses, distresses, disturbs, or worries us, contracts the blood vessels and impedes the free circulation of the blood. On the other hand whatever makes us happy, whatever excites an enjoyable emotion, relaxes the capillaries and gives freedom to the circulation.

Associated with our fear of disease is our modern day incredible and alarming increase in self-prescribed medicines. The widespread use of these "nerve soothers" and nutritional "panaceas" reflects seriously upon the way we are living and working today. This tendency to a cupboard filled with vitamin and nutritional supplements is virtually inherent in the abnormal tension in which our nerves are continuously strained to the breaking point, where we claim—indeed fear—that we can't "let down," and where we lose the ability to surrender ourselves to normal influences for enjoyment as we daily do battle for a livelihood and happiness.

We lash ourselves with the dual blows of we *must* keep up our capacity for productivity and we *must* find happiness at whatever cost. So we begin finding ourselves depending on stimulants of one sort or another in order to *make* happiness physically possible—to escape our stresses and wrest whatever pleasurable sensations we can from life.

As life makes virtual non-stop workers of us, we fear to lose our sensibility for enjoyment of life. We worry lest long hours and demanding work conditions deprive us happiness. And if our souls cannot or will not replace these fears and worries with true happiness in daily living, then we resort to external means, such as stimulants and stress relaxants to give us the pathological counterfeit of happiness.

We are too much goading our nervous systems and brains to give out something that isn't there. "What," asks Dr. George W. Jacoby, one of American's foremost brain doctors, in an *Evening Post* interview, "is the ultimate physical effect of worry? Why, the same as that of a fatal bullet wound or sword thrust. Worry kills as surely, though not so quickly, as ever gun or dagger did, and more people have died in the last century from sheer worry than have been killed in battle."

"The investigations of the neurologists," he goes on to say, "have laid bare no secret of Nature in recent years more startling and interesting than the discovery that worry kills." This is the final, up-to-date word. "Not only is it known," resumes the great neurologist, counting off his words, as it were, on his fingertips, "that worry kills, but the most minute details of its murderous methods are familiar to modern scientists. It is a common belief of those who have made a special study of the science of brain diseases that hundreds of deaths attributed to other causes each year are due simply to worry. In plain, untechnical language, worry works its irreparable injury through certain cells of the brain life. The insidious inroads upon the system can be best likened to the constant falling of drops of water in one spot. In the, brain it is the insistent, never-lost idea, the single, constant thought, centered upon one subject, which in the course of time destroys the brain cells. The healthy brain can cope with occasional worry; it is the iteration and reiteration of disquieting thoughts which the cells of the brain cannot successfully combat.

"The mechanical effect of worry is much the same as if the skull were laid bare and the brain exposed to the action of a little hammer beating continually upon it day after day, until the membranes are disintegrated and the normal functions disabled. The maddening thought that will not be downed, the haunting, ever-present idea that is not or cannot be banished by a supreme effort of the will, is the theoretical hammer which diminishes the vitality of the sensitive nerve organisms, the minuteness of which makes them visible to the eye only under a powerful microscope. The 'worry,' the thought, the single idea grows upon one as time goes on, until the worry victim cannot throw it off. Through this, one set, or, area of cells is affected. The cells are intimately connected, joined together by little fibers, and they in turn are in close relationship with the cells of the other parts of the brain.

"Worry is itself a species of monomania. No mental attitude is more disastrous to personal achievement, personal happiness, and personal usefulness in the world than worry and its twin brother, despondency. The remedy for the evil lies in training the will to cast off cares and seek a change of occupation, when the first warning is sounded by Nature in intellectual lassitude. Relaxation is the certain foe of worry, and 'don't fret' one of the healthiest of maxims."

But we *do* fret, and we force ourselves onward by artificial means until we use up all our reserves and then have no resisting power when disease or illness comes.

Worry and fear have made more addicts of all kinds—be it of drugs, alcohol, or vitamin and mood calming supplements—than almost any other cause. Anything that will vanish care, relieve the strain of worry and anxiety, anything that will bring peace of mind is what a disturbed, distressed, and anxious humanity is seeking.

Millions stop off at bars on their ways home from work, or have a drink upon coming home, believing that in dong so they will get at least a temporary uplift or relief from the things that trouble them, and that they will then be in a better position to conduct their lives. Few realize that all a drink of whiskey does is paralyze, for the time being, the nerves of the walls of the blood vessels in the brain, thus letting in an additional supply of blood, causing temporary congestion and additional brain stimulus, due to the surplus of brain nutriment floating in the blood, and that this condition must always be followed by a corresponding reaction and mental depression.

"Keep cheerful and don't worry," says the doctor when we leave the office, expressing a universal belief of physicians in the fatal blighting, health-destroying influence of worry. Physicians look upon it as a curse. A day of worry is more exhausting than a week of work. Worry upsets our whole system, happiness keeps it in health and order.

We should be able to dominate our own mentalities—be the masters of our own minds at all times. But how few of us can do this. Consider, for instance, the following story by a reporter:

"In the sudden thunder storm of Independence Day," wrote the correspondent, "we were struck by the contrast between two women, each of whom had had some trying experience with the weather. One came through the rain and hail to take refuge at the railway station, under the swaying and uncertain shelter of an escorting man's umbrella. Her skirts were soaked to the knees, her pink ribbons were limp, the purple of the flowers on her hat ran in streaks down the white silk. And yet, though she was a poor girl and her holiday finery must have been relatively costly, she made the best of it with a smile and cheerful words. The other was well sheltered; but she took the disappointment of her hopes and the possibility of a little spattering from a leaky window with frowns and fault-finding."

How many of us like that last girl, curse the weather, deeming our day already "ruined" because of the inevitable vagaries of nature.

Is it not sad to see a person who is strong in most things become a passive victim to the torturing thoughts which he or she should be able to strangle in an instant?

Jay Cooke, many times a millionaire at the age of fifty-one, at fifty-two practically penniless, went to work again and built another fortune. The last of his three thousand creditors was paid, and the promise of the great financier was fulfilled. To a visitor who once asked him how he regained his fortune, Mr. Cooke replied, "That is simple enough: by never changing the temperament I derived from my father and mother. From my earliest experience in life I have always been of a hopeful temperament, never living in a cloud. I have always had a reasonable philosophy to think that men and times are better than harsh criticism would suppose. I believe that this American world of ours is full of wealth, and that it was only necessary to go to work and find it. That is the secret of my success in life. Always look on the sunny side."

We should be able to detect the character of the guest thoughts which gain access to our minds. We should be able to open or close the gates of our minds—to include or exclude as we choose. We should be of the conviction that worry and anxiety have no more right to darken our lives than wild beasts have to live in our homes—that they are just as much out of place. "My body must walk the earth," said an ancient poet, "but I can put wings on my soul and plumes to my hardest thought."

The other day I came across this sentence which struck me quite forcefully: "If you cannot be happy when you are miserable, you cannot be happy at all." The writer no doubt meant that if we allow ourselves to be a victim of our moods, if we cannot command our mental outlook, if we are not the masters of our selves, but go up and down with the mood that happens to be upon us at the moment, then we cannot control our happiness. Such people will not be able to tell you whether they are going to be happy or not, because *they do not know themselves* how they will feel at any particular time.

It is a strange thing that after all the centuries of experience and enlightenment, the human race has not learned that so much of our fears are nothing but a ghost of the imagination, and has not resolved positively to refuse to be tortured by this enemy of happiness. It seems as though the race could have found some way out of this needless suffering centuries ago, but we are still frightened by the same ghosts of fear and worry that haunted our ancestors.

It is strange that that which so often has no basis in reality, which is purely a mental product, a bogy of the imagination—which is what virtually all fear is—should torture so many from the very dawn of history to the present.

Look back upon your life and you will find that your fear of things robbed you of your joy, was, more often than not, of things which never really happened.

"My children," said a dying man, "during my long life I have had a great many troubles, most of which never happened."

A prominent business man in Philadelphia said that his father worried for twenty-five years over an anticipated misfortune which never arrived.

Those who have learned the true art of living will not waste their energies on friction—which accomplishes nothing, but merely grinds out the machinery of life.

"Difficulties melt away before the person who carries about a cheerful spirit and persistently refuses to be discouraged, while they accumulate before the one who is always groaning over his or her hard luck and scanning the horizon for clouds not yet in sight."

Stress is seldom the result of present trouble or work, but of work and trouble anticipated. Mental exhaustion comes from those who look ahead and climb mountains before reaching them.

"We would count a man insane who took a dose of poison every day to promote his health. He is no less mentally unbalanced who desires happiness and yet indulges a habit of worrying."

What would you think of a person who continually spent more than he or she earned, forced to resort less and less on actual available capital and more and more on invisible, extended credit? Your brain power, your creative ability, your energy, are your capital, with which you are to solve your life's problems, and yet, every sleepless night you spend worrying over your affairs, every moment of anxiety, of fretting and stewing, and nervous tension, is draining, off your precious capital. Your brain capital, nerve capital, vitality capital, which should help you to clear up your perplexing problems, you are not only squandering, but in the process you are making yourself and those around you unhappy, destroying the harmony of your home, committing suicide upon months, and, perhaps, years of your life.

Why is it, therefore, that in the face of all of this, most of us are not more capable of happiness?

There ought to be something in each of our lives which is beyond the reach of accident, beyond the possibility of being wrecked by chance. We certainly has an inherent right to success and happiness that is inalienable. We were made to dominate our environment. It was not intended that we should be buffeted about by accident or chance. Our greatest enemies live in our own brains, in our imaginations, in our wrong ideas of life. We were intended to be conquerors instead a slaves, and there is no slavery like that person who is a slave to a conviction or a superstition that makes him or her cowardly.

Foolish superstitions and ignorance mar the happiness of a multitude of people. Many think that superstitions are harmless, but nothing is harmless which makes people believe that they are puppets of circumstances, that they are at the mercy of signs and symbols, that something might be at work against their mortal beings or destinies. When people believe that they are the victims of a destiny which they cannot control, that they are liable at any moment to have their life plans upset, all their hopes frustrated without warning—in other words, that there is no certainty for the future in their endeavors, however great—they cannot develop that solidity of character, that enduring, underlying principle, which is the backbone of every great life.

The trouble is that we do not look within for the mainspring of power. All the time we are depending upon things outside of ourselves to give us peace of mind—comfort, happiness, success. But these things are subject to accident, and we are risking all that life ought to mean to us in pinning our faith to things which are outside our control.

The moment we depend upon outside help, we cut ourselves off from our source of power; we sever the divine cable—no longer drawing our power from the divine current. We try to propel ourselves through the vicissitudes of life without looking our higher nature—without connecting our life-giving generators of faith and truth to the divine current.

There must be a conviction that there is something within us which sustains us under all circumstances, before we can develop an enduring character. There must be a feeling of absolute security, before we can attain that symmetry or arrive at that perfect balance or poise of character which constitutes real manhood and womanhood. As long as there is any doubt in our minds as to whether we are part of the eternal principle—part of the great Infinite plan which cannot be annihilated but is beyond the reach of want, chance, or misfortune—our characters will be defective. They will lack that enduring strength which is characteristic of all great lives.

Fear and worry can only arise in the experience of ourselves as separate from an Infinite principle and supply of love, of truth, and of Omnipotent power.

Life will take on a new meaning when we come into the realization of the unity of everything in the universe, the oneness of all life, and our *at-one-ment* with the great, creating, sustaining Principle of the universe. The idea that there is but one principle running through the universe, one life, one truth, one reality, that this power is divinely beneficent, and that we are really in a great current running Godward, heavenward, is one of the most inspiring, encouraging, and fear-killing truths that has ever entered the human mind. It solves the greatest mysteries of life and gives us a wonderful sense of safety and contentment, which nothing else can give.

In proportion as we realize our oneness with the all of life and the divine principle within it, do our lives become calm, confident creative. God's children are not the victims of chance, are not the playthings of a cold, cruel destiny beyond their control.

Our sense of fear is always in proportion to our sense of weakness or inability to protect ourselves from the cause of it. Our fear, our worry, our anxiety, then, are indications that we have lost consciousness of our divine connection and have strayed from home—that we are out of tune with the Infinite, in discord with divine Principle.

"Every moment of worry weakens the soul for its daily combat," writes a well-known preacher. "Worry is an infirmity; there is no virtue in it. Worry is spiritual nearsightedness; a fumbling way of looking at little things, and of magnifying their value."

There is no worse tyrant than the demon worry. He is, however, a master of our own choosing, as he cannot force his rule upon us against our will.

We are challenged today to overcome worry, but this takes us back to the ancient fight with fear. Fear must go. Yet, through long conflict we have not been able to crush his citadel or drive him from his powerful seat. He continues to hold sway, the arch-enemy of the race, the great robber baron who plunders our hard-hoarded store of human happiness and efficiency.

It is high time we realized that he is not to be forced off his throne by crude attack. Instead, we must, unknown to him, invite in another stronger than he. As Fear works havoc with the imagination, so must this newcomer absorb our thoughts and feelings in a yet stronger way, until at length he draws to himself the allegiance we have so long given Fear. He shall be Fear's antidote—and his name is Faith.

When we have given our allegiance to Faith then shall we see Fear toppling from his ancient throne. We cannot drag him off by force, but we can push him aside little by little to make room for a greater master of the human spirit than he. Where Fear dries up the very source of life, the love that casteth out fear has just the opposite effect.

And when Fear shall be no more, worry, too, shall leave us—both the old enemy and the new disease, the twin enemies of happiness. Then we shall find a sublime, new self-faith. We shall rest in such sense of security, freedom, ability, as we cannot now conceive, as we shall partake of the divine creative power.

It used to be that a melancholy solemnity was regarded as a sign of spirituality, but there is no true religion in it. When we learn that discord, disease, and all that worries and frets and makes us anxious are only the absence of harmony, and that they are not realities of being, that God never made them, and hence they must be false—that only the real, the good, is true, because God made it, and that everything else is false because He did not make it—then we shall learn the secret of real harmonious living, we shall learn the secret of scientific living. Then we can throw the best of ourselves into the most unfortunate environment, we can fling out the fragrance and beauty of serene and balanced lives, even in the most discordant surroundings.

Think the good; drive away evil; keep the mind so filled with the good, the beautiful and the true, that the opposites will find no affinity there. When we learn that there is enough divinity in us to conquer all the inharmonious, to swallow all the discord that would mar the great divine symphony, then we shall be living to some purpose. This knowledge is the magic which will transform the hovel into a palace.

Yes, there are in truth certain events which come upon us unawares, certain psychic states which we cannot foresee nor escape. But once we are conscious of those moods, however, we can, with our remembrance that we are part of the omnipotent oneness of life, become master of them.

The important thing is to keep our physical, mental, and moral standards high, so that worry, anxiety, fear germs cannot get a footing in our system. Our resisting power ought to be so great that it would be impossible for these enemies to get into the mind or body.

I knew a most estimable man who had been terribly handicapped all his life by fear. It had played great havoc with his career. He said that fear had dogged his steps from infancy, had strangled his self-expression, had stood in the way of everything he has ever attempted. It had kept him from undertaking things which he was perfectly, confident he could carry out.

For all his life he has fought desperately against it, not knowing until recently that it he had within himself the power to neutralize it.

Since he found out how to neutralize this great destroyer of his peace, his happiness, and his success, his whole life completely changed. He said he never discovered himself, or truly allowed himself to dream of his possibilities, until he annihilated fear. Now, where he was once weak, timid, vacillating, fearing to undertake things, he is now strong, vigorous, confident. The destruction of fear has unlocked his latent energy and resulted in a tremendous increase of mental power. He can accomplish more now in a month, and easily, than he could have accomplished formerly in a year, and that with very painful effort.

We all can do likewise. We can all turn the darkest experiences into happiness.

And there is no joy equal to that of conquering worry, of overcoming fear.

In such victory, we shall find a happiness beyond all our dreams of happiness.

Today I will…

- *Make it a habit to not think of worrisome thoughts after a certain time in the evening that I decide upon—and that is a sufficient distance from the time I go to bed. "I have made it a rule of my life," said a prominent English clergyman, "never to think of anything disagreeable after nine o'clock at night." Tonight, begin to set aside a time after which you will not permit yourself any disagreeable thoughts.*

- *Remind myself that courage and cheerfulness are within our own will power; moreover, they are my source of safety, and self-preservation. Remind yourself that with faith in your oneness with the omnipotent, universal Principle of life, you can always have courage in the face of any seeming adversity.*

Then you will feel neither a victim of your circumstances nor moods, and cheerfulness will always be your ever available companion.

- *Take a look at the energy I devote to worries that sap my hope and fortitude. In the midst of your expenditure of worrisome energy, ask yourself how much more life, enthusiasm, and energy you would have if you applied that same energy to dealing with the actual issues you have at hand in this moment. Convert as much of your energy as you can into power and moral sunshine.*

- *Remind myself that in the past, no matter what has happened to me, I have survived, prevailed. It's important to remember that no matter what problems you're facing now, you've faced problems of equal or greater magnitude in the past, and overcame them. Trust in that same survival center within you, and calling upon it instead of calling up your worries, write down possible solutions to how you'll respond to, overcome, the worrisome events that is currently in your life.*

- *Learn to recognize the difference between real worries and fears and imaginary ones—and stop scaring myself with the imaginary ones. We all worry too much, and we all worry too much about events that more often than not don't occur, or don't occur with the severity we feared, or that we can't stop from occurring. Pay attention the real worries in your life, and then notice how many times you frighten yourself with imaginary worries. One way to begin confronting these latter worries is to tell yourself "Stop!" (or "Halt!" or "Delete!" or whatever word works for you) every time you catch yourself beginning to give expression to some imagined fear, e.g., "Oh, my god, my check didn't come in the mail today; the phone company is going to shut off my phone!"; "Oh, my god, I made such a fool of myself, he/she will never call me again!"; "Oh, no, I'm running late; they're going to fire me!"; "My father (mother, grandfather, grandmother, etc.) died of this disease when he/she was 53, I wonder if I'll die then, too!";*

etc. Don't let yourself complete these thoughts. Vehemently say "Stop!" to yourself the moment you hear yourself beginning to express them. Some people refer to this as "'Stop' thinking." Quite likely, the thought will return seconds later. Be patient with yourself—you're not going to end overnight all the years you've been alive and scaring yourself with imaginary worries. But in time, if you say "Stop!" every time you begin imagining a worry or fear, they will cease appearing. In the meantime, after you've said "Stop!" think of what you can do to satisfyingly prevent those worries that have some likelihood of coming true from doing so, e.g., if you are late for work, stop at the next corner and go into a place of business and ask if you could please use their phone for a minute, and call your place of work and let them know you're on your way.

➔ _____
   _____
➔ _____
   _____
➔ _____
   _____
➔ _____
   _____

chapter 26

TURNING THE WATER OF LIFE INTO WINE

*"If it is a dark day, never mind; you will lighten it up.
If it is a bright day, you will add to the brightness. Give a word of cheer,
a kindly greeting and a warm handshake to your friends. If you have
enemies, look up, pass them by, forget and try to forgive. If all of us
would only think how much of human happiness is made
by ourselves, there would be less of human misery."*

"A certain aged woman," begins an article in *The Woman's Home Companion*, "whose face serene and peaceful, seems utterly above the little worries and vexations which torment the average woman and leave lines of care, though trouble has by no means passed her by. The Fretful Woman asked her one day the secret of her happiness; and the beautiful old face shone with joy."

"My dear," she said, "I keep a Pleasure Book."

"A what?"

"A Pleasure Book. Long ago I learned that there is no day so dark and gloomy that it does not contain some ray of light, and I have made it one business of my life to write down the little things which mean so much to a woman. I have a book marked for every day of every year since I left school. It is but a little thing: the new gown, the chat with a friend, the thoughtfulness of my husband, a flower, a book, a walk in the field, a letter, a concert, or a drive; but it all goes into my Pleasure Book, and, when I am inclined to fret, I read a few pages to see what a happy, blessed woman I am. You may see my treasures if you will."

"Slowly the peevish, discontented woman turned over the book her friend brought her, reading a little here and there. One day's entries ran thus: 'Had a pleasant letter from mother. Saw a beautiful lily in a window. Found the pin I thought I had lost. Saw such a bright, happy girl on the street. Husband brought some roses in the evening.'"

"Bits of verse and lines from her daily reading have gone into the Pleasure Book of this world-wise woman, until its pages are a storehouse of truth and beauty."

"Have you found a pleasure for every, day?" the Fretful Woman asked.

"For every day," the low voice answered; "I had to make my theory come true, you know."

The Fretful Woman ought to have stopped there, but did not; and she found that page where it was written—"He died with his hand in mine, and my name upon his lips."

Would it not be well for more of us to follow this dear old lady's example and keep Pleasure Book?

"Blessed are the joy makers."

Fortunately for the world there are people who take a delight in mere living, who look upon life as a priceless gift, who delight in their work; who really enjoy everybody and everything, and who always give you the impression that they feel that they were born just in the best time, and in the best place in the world.

"The cheerful person carries perpetually, in his or her presence and personality, an influence that acts upon others as summer warmth on the fields and forests. It wakes up and calls out the best that is in them. It makes them stronger, braver, and happier. Such a person makes a little spot of this world a lighter, brighter, warmer place for other people to live in. To meet this person in the morning is to get inspiration which makes all the day's struggles and tasks easier. His or her hearty handshake puts a thrill of new vigor into your veins. After talking with this person for a few minutes, you feel an exhilaration of spirits, a quickening of energy, a renewal of zest and interest in living, and are ready for any duty or service."

It was said that soldiers in hospitals in the Crimean War used to say they could feel when Florence Nightingale was coming, long before they could see her. They could feel her refined personality, her sweet influence radiating everywhere.

We all know sweet, cheerful, inspiring characters who have the wonderful faculty of turning the common water of life into the most delicious wine. Their presence is a tonic which invigorates, which helps us to bear our burdens. Their advent in the home seems like the coming of the sun after a long arctic night. They unlock the tongue, and we speak with the gift of prophecy. They are marvelous health promoters.

I know a girl who, when she grew to full consciousness of her ugliness of body, her unattractiveness of person, resolved to make herself so beautiful in character, in manner, so cultivated in all that makes life worth living, that people would forget her physical handicaps. She has the most irregular features, a turned-up nose, is cross-eyed, has a very large mouth and an very unattractive figure. Yet she has completely overcome what most girls so consider a fatal handicap that they would probably become morose, pessimistic, disagreeable, and drag out a most unhappy existence—and everybody who knows her loves her. Nobody looks at what she thought would be the great barrier to her popularity. By the cultivation of a gracious, sweet manner, and patience and discipline, she has so transformed herself that one is unconscious of her physical defects. The moment she speaks you are charmed, there is an inexplicable something about her manner which captivates you. It is more than a match for beauty; it is expression of a kindly heart. She makes you feel that she has a real personal interest in you.

Hers is a real beauty that is not evident only for a few years and then leaves one empty and unattractive. It will not fade in time, as it is an expression of spirit which time cannot tarnish or erase; it is not ephemeral as mere physical beauty is, and it attainable by us all. It is a beauty which will enrich everybody who comes in contact with you. It is a beauty which you can carry with you into old age. Or rather, it is a beauty which will drive away old age, for with a sunny heart, a mind which is always cheerful and hopeful and sympathetic, age has little in common.

An old farmer was once asked at a meeting of the Agricultural Congress to give his opinion on the best slope of land for the raising of a particular kind of fruit. "It does not make so much difference," said the old man, "about the slope of the land, as the slope of the man."

Happiness does not depend so much upon our being favorably environed as upon the slope of our mind.

"I see our brother, who has just been ill, lives on Grumbling Street," said a keen-witted Yorkshire man. "I lived there myself for some time, and never enjoyed good health. The air was bad, the house bad, the water bad; the birds never came and sang in the street, and I was gloomy and sad enough. But I 'flitted.' I got into Thanksgiving avenue; and ever since then I have had good health, and so have all my family. The air is pure, the house good; the sun shines on it all day; the birds always singing; and I am as happy as I can be. Now, I recommend our brother to 'flit.' There are plenty of houses to let on Thanksgiving avenue; he will find himself a new man if he will only come, and I shall be right glad to have him for a neighbor."

A lady who was recently asked how she managed to get along so well with disagreeable people said: "It is very simple. All I do is to try to make the most of their good qualities and pay no attention to the disagreeable ones." The people who help us most are those who, like this lady, ignore, or rather try to eradicate, our faults, by drawing out and emphasizing our better qualities and attuning our minds to high ideals.

Few people are large enough to rise above their aches and pains and disappointments. The majority are always talking about them, projecting their dark shadows into your atmosphere, cutting off your sunshine with their clouds. Their ailments and their hard luck and misfortunes seem to be the biggest things about them. You never meet them but they thrust them into your presence.

Those who are not able to rise above the things that trouble them, who cannot overtop their aches and pains, annoyances and disappointments, so that they are of little consequence in comparison with their great life aim, will never become really happy. When these things are not borne heroically, they mar our characters and leave their ugly traces on our faces. Their hideous forms appear in our characters and disfigure our whole lives.

There is an unwritten law among those who are thoroughbred—the to-the-manner-born gentleman and ladies—which compels them to keep their troubles, their ailments, their sorrows, their worries, their losses, to themselves. There is a fine discipline in this! It mellows the character and sweetens the life.

Learn to consume your own smoke. If you have misfortunes, pains, diseases, losses, keep them to yourself. Bury them. Those who know you have them will love you and admire you infinitely more for this suppression. Resolve that you are too large to be overcome by trifles; that you will be larger than the things that tend to annoy you; that you will overtop them with your gladness and cheerfulness. A stout heart and persistent cheerfulness will be more than a match for all your troubles.

In one of Goethe's stories, there is a description of the poor fisherman's hut which was glorified by the light of a little silver lamp. Everything in the hut—the doors, roof, floors, furniture—was transformed into silver by the magic of the silver lamp. So too, a single ray of emotional sunlight can transform every corner of many a poverty-stricken soul with brightness and good cheer.

I know a lady who has been confined to her couch in a small room for years, and can see only the tops of trees from her resting place, yet she is so cheerful and hopeful that people go to her with their troubles and always go away comforted and encouraged.

"Oh, isn't the spring beautiful!" (or summer, autumn, or winter, as the case may be) is her exclamation to callers, even when her body is quivering with pain. Her eyes are always smiling.

Will any one say that this woman, who has brought light and cheer to all who know her, is poor, or a failure simply because she has been confined to that little room all these years? No; she is a greater success than many a rich woman. She has the wealth that is worthwhile—the wealth that survives pain, sorrow, and disasters of all kinds; that does not burn up; which floods or droughts cannot affect—the inexhaustible wealth of a sunny, cheerful soul.

Kindness of heart, charity, helpfulness, unselfishness, love, honesty, sincerity, simplicity, sympathy—these are the most desirable things in life. These are the things we are all trying to get. If we do not have them ourselves, we are trying to get close to those who do possess them.

To save the life of a girl whom he had never seen before, Willie Rough, a crippled newsboy of Gary, Indiana, offered to give his withered leg for skin grafting. The young woman was discharged from the hospital cured, but the anesthetic given to Rough before the operation had been too much for his weak lungs; pneumonia developed and death resulted.

As death stiffened his fingers, a rose, given him by the girl for whom he was sacrificing his life, fell from his hand upon the coverlet of the hospital cot.

"I'm glad," he had whispered a few minutes before the end. "Tell her that—that I'm jes' glad."

And then when his foster-mother knelt beside the bed and hid her face in the edge of the boy's pillow, he reached out a weak hand and stroked her hair.

"Don't cry, Mammy," he begged. "I never 'mounted to nothin' before, and now you know I done sampan' far somebody."

Conscious to the last, he kept smiling, while the nurse and the surgeon in the room, filled with emotion, turned their faces away to hide their tears.

*"I count this thing to be grandly true,
That a noble deed is a step toward God;
Lifting the soul from the common clod
To a purer air and a broader view."*

What a wonderful world this would be to live in, if we all made a strenuous effort toward the things that make for an unselfish, joyous character! The Golden Rule would everywhere be the law of life.

What ripeness is to an orange, what song is to a lark, what culture and refinement are to the intellect, happiness is to the soul. As vulgarity and ignorance betoken a neglected mind, so unhappiness and misery proclaim the neglected heart. The normal nature will keep strong and fresh the chords that vibrate joy.

"I have told you," says Southey, "of the Spaniard who always put on spectacles when about to eat cherries, in order that the fruit might look larger and more tempting. In like manner I make the most of my enjoyments; and though I do not cast my eyes away from my troubles, I pack them in as small a compass as I can for myself, and never let them annoy others."

We are all richer in happiness material than we think. There are a thousand unrecognized, unutilized wellsprings of joy within us. Just think what those born blind and deaf from birth would get out of the things in your everyday life which seem so common, trivial—even sordid to you. What joy they would get out of the weeds by the roadside, which are distasteful to us, and out of the sounds in the street, which only annoy our ears!

We are all infinitely richer than we think! We need only cultivate our faculties to seize, to appreciate, and to enjoy the multitude of things all about us.

Today I will...

→ *Begin my own "Pleasure Book."*
→ *Give happiness to myself by giving happiness to another.*
→ *Pick something I ordinarily think of as dreary, ordinary, etc., and find something beautiful, worthwhile, in it. Often, we think of our lives as rather mundane. But someone else could come along and find beauty or value in what we have learned to take for granted or look askance upon. Pretend, today, that you are from another country, living in poorer circumstances, and look with those eyes at the things around—in your home, on your drive home from work, etc. Look for what that person might find appreciation in that you have ignored or overlooked.*

→ _____
_____
→ _____
_____
→ _____
_____
→ _____
_____

chapter 27

UNPROFITABLE PESSIMISM

The optimist proclaims that we live in the best of all possible worlds; and the pessimist fears this is true.
—James Branch Cabell

Considering how unprofitable such efforts are, it is surprising how many people make a business of looking for trouble.

No one ever looked for trouble yet without finding plenty of it. This is because one can make trouble of anything if the mind is set that way. It is said that during the development of the West, in the days of rough frontier life, the men who always went armed with pistols, revolvers, and bowie-knives always got into difficulties, while the men who never carried arms, but trusted to their own good sense, self-control, tact, and humor, rarely had trouble.

It is just so with the seekers for ordinary trouble. By constantly holding discouraging, dejected, melancholy, gloomy thoughts, they are in fact inviting to themselves all that depresses and destroys.

Most unhappy people have become so gradually, by forming the habit of unhappiness: complaining about the weather; finding fault with their food, crowded cars, and disagreeable companions or work.

The habit of complaining, of criticizing, of faultfinding or grumbling over trifles, the habit of looking for shadows, is one most unfortunate to contract, especially in early life, for after a while it becomes one's master. All of one's impulses become perverted, until the tendency to pessimism, to cynicism, is chronic.

There are specialists among the trouble-seekers.

Some go looking for disease. They keep on hand antidotes for colds and medicine for every possible ailment—which they are sure will all come sometime. When they take a journey across the continent or to Europe they carry a regular drugstore with them, a remedy for every supposed ill that they are likely to strike. And it is no surprise but that they are always feeling ill, are always having colds, are always catching contagious diseases.

Others, who never anticipate trouble, who are always believing the best instead of the worst, go abroad, never take remedies with them, and rarely have any trouble.

Some people are always snuffing for something unhealthy—something too high, too low, too sunny, or too shady. If they have any little ache or pain, they are sure that it is the onset of some terrible disease. Of course they eventually get the disease, because they looked for it, they anticipated it, they expected it. They would be disappointed if they found they were mistaken. The fact is that the only thing that is wrong is their own minds. What they have fretted about in their minds will with inevitability appear in their bodies. It is only a question of time.

Some trouble-seekers fix on the stomach as the storm-center of misfortune. They have elaborate mental charts of what "agrees with" them and what "disagrees with" them, and are always secretly hoping to be able to find some new indigestible viand. They swallow a bit of dyspepsia with every mouthful of food, for they feel sure that everything they eat will hurt them. Of course their suspicious thoughts, their fear thoughts, react upon their digestion, demoralizing the gastric juice or preventing its secretion entirely, and, of course, there is trouble.

Some of these peculiar individuals find the air the most prolific source of their quarry. If the bedroom window is left open, they warn against pneumonia, colds, and sudden death. Indeed, if there is a window open *anywhere*, these suspecters of aerial mischief expect a cold, and are sure to get it. But it is their very fear, their very anxiety, that demoralizes the natural resisting power of their bodies and makes it susceptible.

If there is a contagious disease anywhere in the neighborhood, the trouble-expecters are sure to contract it. If one of their children coughs or has a little too much color in the cheek, or does not feel hungry, they are certain that some dreaded disease must be beginning its deadly work.

The saddest cases of all, perhaps, are those who have a fixed idea that some disease, usually supposed to be inherited, will ultimately kill them. The self-convinced victims of weak lungs, weak hearts, or weak stomachs brood and dwell upon their threatened physical disasters, causing them to throw their pall over every activity. All that such people need to be well and happy is a better mental state, a buoyant, hopeful attitude and the activity that would come with such a philosophy. Instead, they are the prey of quacks of every kind, and swallow millions of gallons of concoctions whose advertisements fill newspapers and magazines with promises of amazing preventive and curative promises. They support many a fashionable physician in luxury, and make their lives tenfold more miserable than by any standard of right it ought to be.

Certain other people are always complaining of their hard lot and poverty. They go about with disaster written on their very faces. They are walking advertisements of their own failures—always talking, but never doing.

I know a bright, energetic young man who has started in business for himself, but who has formed a most unfortunate habit of talking down about his business to everybody. When anybody asks him how his business is getting along he says, "Poorly, poorly; no business; doing absolutely nothing; just barely making a living; no money in it; I wish I could sell out; I made a great mistake in going into this line of business; I would have been a great deal better off on salary." This man has formed such a habit of talking his business down that even when business is good, he still calls it poor. He radiates a discouraging atmosphere, he flings out discouraging suggestions, and makes you feel tired and disgusted that a young man of such promise and such possibilities should so drown his prospects and strangle his ambition.

This habit is especially unfortunate in an employer, because it is contagious. It destroys the confidence of the employees in the employer and the business. People do not like to work for a pessimist. They thrive in a cheerful, optimistic atmosphere, and will do more and better work there than in one of discouragement and depression.

Those who talk their business down cannot possibly do so well as those who talk theirs up. The habit of talking everything down sets the mind toward the negative side, the destructive side, instead of toward the positive and creative, and is fatal to achievement. It creates a discordant environment.

No one can live upward when he or she is talking downward.

The imagination, wrongly used, is one of our worst foes. I know people who live in perpetual unhappiness and discomfort because they imagine they are being abused, slighted, neglected, and talked about. They think themselves the target for all sorts of evils, the object of envy, jealousy, and all kinds of ill will. More often than not, most of their concerns are delusions and have no reality whatever.

Negativity is a most unfortunate state of mind to get into. It kills happiness, it demoralizes usefulness, it throws the mind out of harmony, and life itself becomes unsatisfactory. People who clutch onto negative thoughts make themselves perpetually wretched by surrounding themselves with an atmosphere reeking with pessimism. They always wear dark glasses, which make everything around them seem draped in mourning; they see nothing but darkness. All the music of their lives is set to the minor key; there is nothing cheerful or bright in their world. They have talked poverty, failure, hard luck, fate, and hard times so long that their entire being is imbued with pessimism. The cheerful qualities of the mind have atrophied from neglect and disuse, while their pessimistic tendencies have been so overdeveloped that their minds cannot regain a normal, healthy, cheerful balance. With them, times are always hard, money scarce, and the world "going to the dogs." Nobody likes to converse with them, because they are always telling their stories of hard luck and misfortune. People avoid them as they would miasmatic swamps—full of chills and fever.

A most injurious and unpleasant way of looking for trouble is fault-finding, continual criticism of other persons. Some people are never generous, never magnanimous toward others. They are stingy of their praise, showing always an unhealthy parsimony in their recognition of merit in others, and critical of their every act.

A great many other people think they would be happy if they were only in different circumstances, when the fact is that circumstances have little, if anything, to do with one's temperament or disposition to enjoy the world.

I know people who have lost their best friends, who have all their lives been apparently unfortunate, have struggled against odds and have themselves been invalids, and yet they have borne up bravely through it all, and have been cheerful, hopeful, inspiring to all who knew them.

Those who are always grumbling about their circumstances, hard luck, and poverty, should be mindful that thousands of people would be happy in precisely their condition.

There are times that I wish that I had the power to stir the inmost soul of all these people to realize how much their own fate lies in the control of their own thoughts, but "To help a person who is at 'outs' with everything and everybody," writes George C. Tenney, from experience in a sanatorium, "is like trying to save a drowning person who is determined to drown."

Don't go through life looking for trouble, for faults, for failures, for the crooked, the ugly, and the deformed. Make up your mind that you will not criticise or condemn others, or find fault with their mistakes and shortcomings. Fault-finding, indulging in sarcasm and irony, picking flaws in everything and everybody, looking for things to condemn instead of to praise, is a very dangerous habit to oneself. It is like a deadly worm which gnaws at the heart of the rosebud or fruit, and will make your own life gnarled, distorted, and bitter.

No life can be harmonious and happy after this blighting habit is once formed. Those who always look for something to condemn ruin their own characters and destroy their normal integrity.

It is just as easy to go through life looking for the good and the beautiful, instead of the ugly; for the noble instead of the ignoble; for the bright and cheerful instead of the dark and gloomy; for the hopeful instead of the despairing; for the bright side instead of the dark side. To set your face always toward the sunlight is just as easy as to see always the shadows, and it makes all the difference in your life, between prosperity and adversity, between, success and failure—and in your character between content and discontent, happiness and misery

Learn to look for the light. Positively refuse to harbor shadows. Hold to those things that give pleasure, that are helpful and inspiring.

If you have been in the habit of talking down your business, the times, your friends, and everything, just reverse the process, talk everything up, and see how soon your changed thought will change the atmosphere about you and improve your conditions.

The strong, the positive, do not allow themselves to talk and think negatives. They do not say "I can't," but "I can." They do not say "I will try the thing," but "I will do it." "Cant's" have ruined more boys and girls, men and women than almost anything else, for to get into the negative habit, the doubting habit, tends to keep them down. They are fastening bonds of servitude around themselves, and will not be able to counteract their influence unless they reverse their thinking, talking, and acting.

The balanced soul is never suspicious and does not expect trouble. Quite the reverse.

The balanced soul knows that darkness is only the forerunner of approaching light.

Keep yourself in balance, and life will appear to you as it truly is.

And equanimity and contentment will always be your companions.

Today I will…

- *Examine the ways I may be taking a pessimistic view of things and contributing to my own unhappiness.*

- *Look at how I may be unwittingly adding to the world's and my own discontentment by priding myself in finding faults. We have all been so subject to criticism that it is easier for most of us to find the shortcomings, mistakes, inconsistencies, etc. in things, and then praising ourselves for our cleverness, perceptiveness, discernment. There is good in seeing the errors in things, but are we doing so to the exclusion of being able to see and express the good?*

- *If criticizing someone, also find something complimentary to say. Instead of saying, "You did a terrible job with that assignment," or "You didn't do what I asked you," preface your comments by saying something complimentary, as most likely the other person wasn't trying to discomfit you. Instead of saying, for example, "You did a terrible job with that assignment," say, "I can see that you put your best effort into trying to make this assignment right. And that's great. There are things we must do now to carry forward your efforts so that they are truly successful." Then you can proceed to point out the places where the assignment fell short.*

→ _____

→ _____

→ _____

→ _____

chapter 28

YOUR MOST VALUABLE POSSESSION

*"But how shall we expect charity towards others
when we are uncharitable to ourselves?"*
—*Sir Thomas Browne*

Nothing else is worth so much to you as your unqualified endorsement of yourself. The approval of "the still, small voice" within you, which says to every noble act, "That is right," and to every ignoble one, "That is wrong," is worth more to you than all the kingdoms of earth. It matters little what others may think about you or what the world may say; it makes no difference whether the press or the public praises or blames; it is by your own honest judgment of yourself that you must stand or fall.

There is no alchemy by which a person who has not earned his or her own approval can extract real happiness and true satisfaction from either money or position.

"When a person does not find repose in himself," says a French proverb, "it is vain to seek it elsewhere."

Be sure, then, that you have your own approval first and last. Resolve that you will never forfeit confidence in yourself and that you will never take chance of your own disapproval, whatever you have or do not have, and you will have a bulwark which will be your stay whether in prosperity or adversity.

At the least murmur of disapproval of the "still, small voice," halt and ask yourself what you are about to do and whither you are going. There is something wrong—of that you may be sure. You must remedy it immediately. Don't parley with the cause of your disturbance; don't try to compensate with it. Such a course will prove as dangerous as that of a mariner who, in the midst of a storm, would insist upon holding the needle to a certain point by force because he wanted to sail in that direction. To try to influence the compass would be to wreck his ship onto the rock and shoals of his path. There are human wrecks all along the ocean of life who have disregarded or tried to compromise with the compass of their conscience.

To keep your self-approval you must be honest. It is impossible to be dishonest and not stand condemned before the bar of conscience. No matter how slight the departure from truth or integrity, no matter how trifling the deception of untruthfulness (if any deception or untruthfulness can be considered slight), you have been tampering with the needle, and, if you persist in such a course, you will not reach the harbor you seek.

You cannot sell shoddy for all wool, thirty-two inches for a yard, thirty quarts for a bushel, or domestic for imported goods; you cannot cheat your employer of time or service or by not giving the best that is in you, without compromising with your conscience. It is impossible to do an unethical act —however secretly, and although no one in the world may see or know it— without a corresponding deterioration of your character.

If you keep your self-approval, no matter what other things you may lose, you will still be rich. You may make a fortune or you may lose one; you may live in a beautiful home or in a cheap boarding-house; you may wear rich garments or cheap ones; you may ride in a fine car of your may walk; you may keep your friends or you may lose them; you may have the good opinion of the world or its contempt, but, if you have never tampered with our conscience, if you believe in yourself, if you approve of your life, if you have been honest and earnest and true, and if you can look yourself square in the face without wincing, you will be happy and successful, even though the world should brand you as a failure.

Today I will…

- *Pay attention to the voice within me that cautions me when I am violating my sense of self. How often do we feel that twinge of conscience but ignore it, later to regret having done so. Learn to trust it. Sometimes it may indeed by incorrect. That's okay. In the long run it's better to trust yourself and err in your actions—we all, after all, make mistakes—than to doubt yourself, fail to heed yourself. It's easier to correct an erroneous act, than an erroneous spirit.*

- *Learn to develop the skill to listen to my inner voice. One technique for doing this is to first think of something that you know to be absolutely true—as the memory of the first person you loved. Devote all your attention to the thought of this situation. See the truth of it, relive the truth of it. While doing so, examine where in your body you're feeling the truth of it, and pay attention to that feeling. Then take that experience and deny it. Notice what happens now in that place inside your body where you felt its truth a moment ago. Now know what the feeling of truth is in your body, and you have a way of determining whether something you're "feeling" is indeed true or not. If when you think about it and visualize it it stirs the identical feeling in that center of truth within you that you felt in this experiment, then you know it's true. If you take that new belief into that center of truth in your body and you feel nothing, or your feel what you felt when you denied your truth in this experiment, then you know that what you're feeling is most likely not true or is not yet convincingly true for you.*

- *Remember that self-approval and self-deception cannot coexist. We can always approve of anything that we do, but genuine self-approval requires that we are acting in accordance with our principles. Write out the core principles you believe in. When you grant yourself self-approval, make sure that it's for an action you performed in allegiance to your principles. If it's not, then in granting yourself self-approval for your actions, you will be betraying your principles. You will be deceiving yourself, and your self-approval will lack integrity and your word will lack trustworthiness. You will then lack the ability to test with confidence the genuineness of that inner voice that is guiding you.*

→ _____
_____
→ _____
_____
→ _____
_____
→ _____
_____

chapter 29

THE CRIME OF SELF-DEPRECIATION

*If the Supreme Creator had meant us to be gloomy,
he would, it seems to me, have clothed the earth in black,
not in that lively green, which is the livery of cheerfulness and joy.*
—Janet Graham, Scottish poet and author

One of the most demoralizing things we witness is another's habit of berating himself or herself. Some people are always doing this. They seem to delight in telling how little they amount to, and how insignificant they are in comparison with others.

Ironically, and sadly, the churches are largely responsible for much of our self-depreciation. How often we hear in prayer-meetings this constant berating of one's self! People call themselves miserable sinners, poor worms of the dust, instead of kings and queens—the men and women God made. Clergymen in pulpits and people in prayer-meetings often tell the Lord how insignificant they are. Instead of boldly claiming their birthright of nobility, of royal manhood and womanhood, they whine and apologize and crawl. Human beings were created erect that they might stand up, look up, look the world in the face without wincing. If the Bible teaches anything it bids us to look up, to claim our birthright. This acting the Uriah Heep before the Creator is despicable and demoralizing.

The habit of self-depreciation is demoralizing to one's character. It destroys self-confidence, kills independence and makes one vertebrateless. What would a parent think of a child who approached with a request in a humiliating spirit of self-depreciation?

Some people seem to have a regular genius for self-effacement. They skulk round, always trying to keep in the back seats or out of sight as much as possible wherever they go.

There is something in human nature which despises sneaking.

"No man," says Emerson, "can be cheated out of an honorable career in life unless he cheats himself."

Do not carry with you in life a small contemptible estimate of yourself. A noble estimate of life and of one's self is a powerful projector of character. You will not cheat yourself unless you cease to believe in yourself.

And nor will you cheat others.

Self-respect, a good opinion of your own personality, is the best insurance against vicious tendencies and wrong choices: Those who think highly of themselves will not stoop to underhanded methods, to scheming.

One reason you may have failed to assert yourself is perhaps because you have been disgusted with nervy people who substituted cheek for ability, and you determined to assume a non-pretentious, humble air; but self-effacement never yet made person out of a human being, and never will. There is much difference between disagreeable, bragging conceit based upon cheap vanity or false pride, and real confidence based upon a knowledge of ability and honest conviction that we are capable of doing the thing we undertake.

Remember, the world loves those who have the courage to stand erect, to think their own thoughts, to live their own lives, and to call themselves every inch a human being. No matter what your calling, therefore, preserve your self-respect at all hazards.

Let your money go, let your property go, part with everything material —but hold onto your self-respect.

Shakespeare said it all in a few, simple words …

"This above all: to thine own self be true."

Today I will…

- *Remind myself that not matter what I do, to like myself. If you struggle with insecurity, lack of self-worth, practice repeating "I like myself" as often a day as you can. Every time you do something and you begin to chastise yourself, stop and say "I like myself." You may have to do this hundreds of times a day. That's okay. It's better than berating yourself hundreds of times a day. If you repeat "I like myself" persistently, eventually you will find that you will stop berating yourself. The voice that berates you will so often be interrupted by your saying "I like myself," that in time it will cease speaking altogether—just like we do if we find that we are always being interrupted by someone. What's important to keep in mind, here, is that saying that you like yourself isn't saying that you approve of everything that you do. It just means that at the least, you still value the person who did that thing.*

- *Not compromise myself in order to win the approval of others. If you compromise yourself to get in the good graces of others, to curry their favor, you may win their approval, but you will lose your own. Better to be an outsider with your own self-approval, than an insider with a loss of conscience.*

- *Remind myself that the opposite of self-depreciation is not egotism. Liking yourself is not the same as boasting about yourself, and nor is it the same as thinking of yourself as better than others. It is accepting yourself—unconditionally, without strings attached, and comparing yourself to others (favorably or unfavorably).*

- *Not speak negatively of myself. There are lots of ways in which we deprecate ourselves, and they are not all in vehement self-denunciation. Tripping over something and saying, "Gee, be clumsy or something," or "Coordinated, Bill (or whatever your name)"; doing something silly or incorrect and saying "I'm so dense," after doing it or after someone shows you the correct way to do it; saying "I'm not good at this" rather than "I'll make the time to learn more about how to do this"— these are just some of the many, subtle ways we speak self-*

deprecatingly about ourselves. An interesting, if not startling, experiment is to carry a small notepad around with you and enter into it every time you speak self-deprecatingly about yourself in a day. Ask your friends, colleagues at work, etc, to help you by pointing out to you—and doing so gently—the times you do speak negatively, self-deprecatingly about yourself. If you do this for just three days, you might find yourself filling several notepads! But you'll learn how to catch yourself. Then you can practice "stop thinking." (See the "Today I will..." section at the end of the "The Twin Enemies of Happiness" chapter.)

→ _____
_____
→ _____
_____
→ _____
_____
→ _____
_____

www.ingramcontent.com/pod-product-compliance
Lightning Source LLC
Chambersburg PA
CBHW081720100526
44591CB00016B/2440